THE *Popular Carol Book*

MOWBRAY

1 *A child this day is born*

1 A child this day is born,
  A child of high renown;
  Most worthy of a sceptre,
  A sceptre and a crown.

2 Good news the shepherds heard,
  Who watched their flock and fold;
  The angel that appeared to them
  Of God's salvation told.

3 And what the angel said,
  Did yet in truth appear;
  At Bethlehem they found the child,
  Laid in a manger there.

4 Then glory be to God
  Who reigns supreme on high;
  With glad thanksgiving, worthy praise,
  And joyful melody!

5 Nowell, nowell, nowell,
  Nowell sing all we may,
  Because the King of all kings
  Was born on Christmas day.

English traditional

*The original words came,
like the tune, from
William Sandys's
Christmas Carols,
published in 1833.
Our version is somewhat
shorter than the 21 verses
included there.*

2 *A cry in the night*
(Ballad of the Homeless Christ)

1 A cry in the night
  And a child is born;
  A child in a stable,
  There isn't any room:
  A cry in the night, and God has made
  Our homelessness his home.

2 A trial in the dark,
  The disciples run;
  They bring him to Pilate,
  He stands there all alone:
  A trial in the dark, and God has made
  Our homelessness his home.

3 A man on a cross,
  And the sun beats down;
  Up there on the gallows
  He's got a thorny crown:
  A man on a cross, and God has made
  Our homelessness his home.

Geoffrey Ainger (b. 1925)

*Words and music
© Geoffrey Ainger.
Used by permission of
Stainer and Bell.
USA © 1964, Galliard Ltd.
Used by permission of
Galaxy Music Corp.,
Boston.*

*A carol with an explicit
social message about
homelessness, arising out
of the very poor housing
situation, particularly for
black families, in Geoffrey
Ainger's Notting Hill
parish during the 1960s.
It relates to all homeless*

4 A voice in the dawn
When the women came;
'You're looking for Jesus,
Don't seek him in a tomb':
A voice in the dawn, and God has made
Our homelessness his home.

people everywhere.
'Notting Hill' was
composed by Ian Calvert
(b. 1940), a member of
the same church.

3 *A great and mighty wonder*

1 A great and mighty wonder,
A full and holy cure!
The Virgin bears the Infant
With virgin-honour pure.

    Repeat the hymn again!
    'To God on high be glory,
    And peace on earth shall reign!'

St Germanus (634–734),
tr. John Mason Neale
(1818–66)

A German traditional
carol, whose melody,
harmonized by Michael
Praetorius (1571–1621),
is full of rhythmic interest,
and needs a dancing
lightness in performance.

2 The word becomes incarnate
And yet remains on high!
And cherubim sing anthems
To shepherds from the sky.

    Repeat the hymn again! . . .

3 While thus they sing your Monarch,
Those bright angelic bands,
Rejoice, ye vales and mountains,
Ye oceans clap your hands.

    Repeat the hymn again! . . .

4 Since all he comes to ransom,
By all be he adored,
The Infant born in Bethl'em,
The Saviour and the Lord.

    Repeat the hymn again! . . .

5 And idol forms shall perish,
And error shall decay,
And Christ shall wield his sceptre,
Our Lord and God for ay.

    Repeat the hymn again! . . .

4 *All my heart this night rejoices*

1 All my heart this night rejoices
As I hear,
Far and near,
Sweetest angel voices:
'Christ is born!' their choirs are singing,
Till the air
Ev'rywhere
Now with joy is ringing.

2 Hark! a voice from yonder manger,
Soft and sweet,
Doth entreat,
'Flee from woe and danger!
People, come! from all doth grieve you,
You are freed;
All you need
I will surely give you.'

3 Come, then, let us hasten yonder!
Here let all,
Great and small,
Kneel in awe and wonder!
Love him who with love is yearning!
Hail the star
That from far
Bright with hope is burning!

4 Thee, dear Lord, with heed I'll cherish,
Live to thee,
And with thee,
Dying, shall not perish;
But shall dwell with thee for ever,
Far on high,
In the joy
That can alter never.

Paul Gerhardt (1607–76),
tr. Catherine Winkworth
(1829–78)

Lutheran Paul Gerhardt
lived for the whole of his
youth and early adulthood
through the Thirty Years
War. His many great
hymns, with their mystical
quality, strike a personal
note. In this one we are
all called to the manger.
  'Bonn', by Johann
Georg Ebeling (1637–76),
is of very simple
construction, a pre-Bach
chorale making a
marvellous congregational
anthem.

5 *Angels, from the realms of glory*

1 Angels, from the realms of glory,
Wing your flight o'er all the earth;
Ye who sang creation's story,
Now proclaim Messiah's birth:

  Come and worship
  Christ the new-born King;
  Come and worship,
  Worship Christ, the new-born King.

James Montgomery
(1771–1854) and Anon.

Angels, shepherds, wise
men and saints are
summoned in turn to
come and worship the
new-born King. The final
verse comes originally

2 Shepherds, in the field abiding,
Watching o'er your flocks by night,
God with us is now residing,
Yonder shines the Infant Light:

    Come and worship . . .

3 Sages, leave your contemplations,
Brighter visions beam afar;
Seek the great Desire of Nations,
Ye have seen his natal star:

    Come and worship . . .

4 Saints before the altar bending
Watching long in hope and fear,
Suddenly the Lord, descending,
In his temple shall appear:

    Come and worship . . .

5 Though an infant now we view him,
He shall fill his Father's throne,
Gather all the nations to him;
Every knee shall then bow down:

    Come and worship . . .

from another carol, in The
Christmas Box *(1825).*
*'Come and worship' are
Montgomery's own words
for the refrain, rather than
'Gloria in excelsis Deo',
which belonged to 'Les
anges dans nos
campagnes' (no. 58), the
old French carol which he
was translating. The
Canadian version of this is
no. 90.*

    *The harmony for 'Iris' is
by Martin Shaw
(1875–1958), adapted by
the editors.*

---

6 As Joseph was a-walking, he heard an angel sing (Cherry Tree Carol)

1 As Joseph was a-walking, he heard an angel sing,
This night shall be born our heavenly King.
He neither shall be born in housen nor in hall,
Nor in the place of Paradise, but in an ox's stall.
Noel, Noel.

2 As Joseph was a-walking, he heard an angel sing,
This night shall be born our heavenly King.
He neither shall be clothèd in purple nor in pall,
But all in fair linen as wear babies all.
Noel, Noel.

3 As Joseph was a-walking, he heard an angel sing,
This night shall be born our heavenly King.
He neither shall be rockèd in silver nor in gold,
But in a wooden cradle that rocks on the mould.
Noel, Noel.

English traditional

*Part 2 of 'The Cherry Tree
Carol', once one of the
most popular of all folk
carols, and traditionally
sung on Christmas Eve.
(Part 1 is the legend of
Joseph and Mary talking
in a cherry orchard,
which also appears in the
Coventry Mysteries.)*

    *'Joseph' is by R. R. Terry
(1865–1938), organist at
Westminster Cathedral,
who became very
interested in folk song
revival.*

4 As Joseph was a-walking, he heard an angel sing,
   This night shall be born our heavenly King.
   He neither shall be christenèd in white wine nor in
       red,
   But in the fair spring water, as we were christenèd.
   Noel, Noel.

---

7   *As with gladness men of old*

1 As with gladness men of old
   Did the guiding star behold,
   As with joy they hailed its light,
   Leading onward, beaming bright,
   So, most gracious God, may we
   Evermore be led to thee.

2 As with joyful steps they sped
   To that lowly manger-bed,
   There to bend the knee before
   Him whom heaven and earth adore,
   So may we with willing feet
   Ever seek thy mercy-seat.

3 As they offered gifts most rare
   At that manger rude and bare,
   So may we with holy joy,
   Pure, and free from sin's alloy,
   All our costliest treasures bring,
   Christ, to thee our heavenly King.

4 Holy Jesu, every day
   Keep us in the narrow way;
   And, when earthly things are past,
   Bring our ransomed souls at last
   Where they need no star to guide,
   Where no clouds thy glory hide.

5 In the heavenly country bright
   Need they no created light;
   Thou its Light, its Joy, its Crown,
   Thou its Sun which goes not down:
   There for ever may we sing
   Alleluyas to our King.

*W. Chatterton Dix
(1837– 98)*

*Dix was a businessman
who wrote the hymn in
1860, while recovering
from a serious illness. The
first three verses compare
the journey of the three
wise men (Matthew
2.1–11) to our own
spiritual pilgrimage, and
the hymn ends with
prayer and worship.
   'Dix' is abridged by
W. H. Monk (1823–89)
from a chorale by Conrad
Kocher (1786–1872).*

8 A virgin most pure, as the prophet do tell

1 A virgin most pure, as the prophet do tell,
   Hath brought forth a baby as it hath befel,
   To be our Redeemer from death, hell, and sin,
   Which Adam's transgression had wrappèd us in.

   Aye, and therefore be merry;
   Rejoice, and be you merry;
   Set sorrow aside;
   Christ Jesus our Saviour was born on this tide.

2 At Bethlem in Jewry a city there was,
   Where Joseph and Mary together did pass,
   And there to be taxèd with many one moe,
   For Caesar commanded the same should be so.

   Aye, and therefore be merry; . . .

3 But when they had entered the city so fair,
   A number of people so mighty was there,
   That Joseph and Mary, whose substance was small,
   Could find in the inn there no lodging at all.

   Aye, and therefore be merry; . . .

4 Then were they constrained in a stable to lie,
   Where horses and asses they used for to tie;
   Their lodging so simple they took it no scorn;
   But against the next morning our Saviour was born.

   Aye, and therefore be merry; . . .

5 The King of all kings to this world being brought,
   Small store of fine linen to wrap him was sought;
   But when she had swaddled her young son so
       sweet,
   Within an ox manger she laid him to sleep.

   Aye, and therefore be merry; . . .

6 Then God sent an angel from Heaven so high,
   To certain poor shepherds in fields where they lie,
   And bade them no longer in sorrow to stay,
   Because that our Saviour was born on this day.

   Aye, and therefore be merry; . . .

7 Then presently after the shepherds did spy
   A number of angels that stood in the sky;
   They joyfully talkèd and sweetly did sing,
   To God be all glory, our heavenly King.

   Aye, and therefore be merry; . . .

English traditional

This traditional carol, first printed in 1834, follows St Luke's Nativity story.
    The tune needs to be kept flowing: think of one beat in a bar.

9   *Away in a manger, no crib for a bed*

1 Away in a manger, no crib for a bed,
The little Lord Jesus laid down his sweet head.
The stars in the bright sky looked down where he lay,
The little Lord Jesus asleep on the hay.

2 The cattle are lowing, the baby awakes,
But little Lord Jesus no crying he makes.
I love thee, Lord Jesus! Look down from the sky,
And stay by my side until morning is nigh.

3 Be near me, Lord Jesus; I ask thee to stay
Close by me forever, and love me, I pray.
Bless all the dear children in thy tender care,
And fit us for heaven, to live with thee there.

Lutheran

'Away in a manger' first appeared anonymously in America in 1885. Both words and tune have in the past been mistakenly ascribed to Martin Luther. Verse 3 was added by J. T. McFarland about 1906. It is rather sentimental, but it hits the spot for most of us at Christmas.

  'Cradle Song' was written for these words by the gospel song-writer W. J. Kirkpatrick (1838–1921). It should be sung smoothly, but not too slowly, if possible singing each line in one breath.

10   *Bethlehem, of noble cities*

1 Bethlehem, of noble cities
None can once with thee compare;
Thou alone the Lord from heaven
Didst for us incarnate bear.

2 Fairer than the sun at morning
Was the star that told his birth;
To the lands their God announcing,
Seen in fleshly form on earth.

3 By its lambent beauty guided
See the eastern kings appear;
See them bend, their gifts to offer,
Gifts of incense, gold and myrrh.

4 Solemn things of mystic meaning:
Incense doth the God disclose,
Gold a royal child proclaimeth,
Myrrh a future tomb foreshows.

Prudentius (348–410), tr. Edward Caswall (1814–78)

One of very few ancient hymns to have been handed down from the early Church's celebration of the Epiphany. It reflects the teaching of the early Fathers about the symbolic meaning of the three gifts.

  Another version, beginning 'Earth hath many a noble city', is also sung to 'Stuttgart', a majestic tune by C. F. Witt (1660–1716).

5 Holy Jesu, in thy brightness
To the Gentile world displayed,
With the Father and the Spirit
Endless praise to thee be paid.

11 *Born in the night, Mary's Child*

1 Born in the night, Mary's Child,
A long way from your home;
Coming in need, Mary's Child,
Born in a borrowed room:

2 Clear shining light, Mary's Child,
Your face lights up our way:
Light of the world, Mary's Child,
Dawn on our darkened day.

3 Truth of our life, Mary's Child,
You tell us God is good:
Prove it is true, Mary's Child,
Go to your cross of wood.

4 Hope of the world, Mary's Child,
You're coming soon to reign:
King of the earth, Mary's Child,
Walk in our streets again.

Geoffrey Ainger (b. 1925)

*Words and music ©
Geoffrey Ainger.
Used by permission of
Stainer and Bell.
USA © 1964, Galliard Ltd.
Used by permission of
Galaxy Music Corp.,
Boston.*

*Like 'Ballad of the
Homeless Christ' (no. 2),
a carol inspired by the
social issues faced during
Geoffrey Ainger's 1960s
Notting Hill ministry.*

12 *Brightest and best of the sons of the morning*

1 Brightest and best of the sons of the morning,
Dawn on our darkness and lend us thine aid;
Star of the East, the horizon adorning,
Guide where our infant Redeemer is laid.

2 Cold on his cradle the dew-drops are shining,
Low lies his head with the beasts of the stall:
Angels adore him in slumber reclining,
Maker and Monarch and Saviour of all.

3 Say, shall we yield him, in costly devotion,
Odours of Edom and offerings divine?
Gems of the mountain and pearls of the ocean,
Myrrh from the forest or gold from the mine?

4 Vainly we offer each ample oblation,
Vainly with gifts would his favour secure;
Richer by far is the heart's adoration,
Dearer to God are the prayers of the poor.

*Reginald Heber
(1783–1826)*

*Poetic nature imagery is
used to paint the Nativity
scene in this hymn, first
published in 1811. The
purpose is to make us
imagine the scene and
then think deeply about
what God really wants
from us.
    'Epiphany', by
F. J. Thrupp (1827– 67),
is the most cheerful of the
tunes to which the words
are commonly sung.*

5 Brightest and best of the sons of the morning,
  Dawn on our darkness and lend us thine aid;
  Star of the East, the horizon adorning,
  Guide where our infant Redeemer is laid.

---

13 *Child in the manger*

1 Child in the manger,
  Infant of Mary,
  Outcast and stranger,
  Lord of all!
  Child who inherits
  All our transgressions,
  All our demerits
  On him fall.

2 Once the most holy
  Child of Salvation,
  Gentle and lowly,
  Lived below;
  Now, as our glorious
  Mighty Redeemer,
  See him victorious
  O'er each foe.

3 Prophets foretold him,
  Infant of Wonder;
  Angels behold him
  On his throne;
  Worthy our Saviour
  Of all their praises;
  Happy for ever
  Are his own.

Lachlan Macbean
(1853–1931), after Mary
MacDonald (1789–1872)

The Gaelic melody
'Bunessan' has become
popularly associated with
the words of 'Morning has
broken', and once
reached the hit parade
Top Ten; but it belongs
originally to this carol.

---

14 *Child of Mary, newly born*

1 Child of Mary, newly born,
  Softly in a manger laid,
  Wake to wonder on this morn,
  View the world your fingers made.
  Starlight shone above your bed,
  Lantern-light about your birth:
  Morning sunlight crown your head,
  Light and Life of all the earth!

Timothy Dudley-Smith
(b. 1926)

Words © Timothy
Dudley-Smith. Used by
permission.

It is Christ the young hero
sent from heaven —

2 Child of Mary, grown and strong,
Traveller, teacher, young and free,
See him stride the hills along,
Christ the Man of Galilee.
Wisdom from a world above
Now by waiting hearts is heard:
Hear him speak the words of love,
Christ the true eternal Word.

3 Child of Mary, grief and loss,
All the sum of human woe,
Crown of thorn and cruel cross,
Mark the path you choose to go.
Man of Sorrows, born to save,
Bearing all our sins and pains:
From his cross and empty grave
Christ the Lord of Glory reigns.

4 Child of Mary, gift of grace,
By whose birth shall all be well,
One with us in form and face,
God with us, Emmanuel!
Night is past and shadows fled,
Wake to joy on Christmas morn:
Sunlight crown the Saviour's head,
Christ the Prince of Peace is born.

*almost closer to the
demigod of Greek
mythology than Isaiah's
vision of the suffering
servant —whose birth is
joyfully celebrated in
Bishop Dudley-Smith's
attractive carol.*

*'Lynch's Melody',
arranged by Donald
Dawson from a tune in
J. P. Lynch's* Melodies of
Ireland *(c.1845), is of
appealing simplicity, and
should be sung calmly.*

---

15 *Christians awake! Salute the happy morn*

1 Christians awake! salute the happy morn
Whereon the Saviour of the world was born;
Rise to adore the mystery of love
Which hosts of angels chanted from above;
With them the joyful tidings first begun
Of God incarnate and the Virgin's son.

2 Then to the watchful shepherds it was told,
Who heard the angelic herald's voice, 'Behold,
I bring good tidings of a Saviour's birth
To you and all the nations upon earth:
This day hath God fulfilled his promised word,
This day is born a Saviour, Christ the Lord.'

3 He spake; and straightway that celestial choir
In hymns of joy, unknown before, conspire;
The praises of redeeming love they sing,
And heaven's whole orb with alleluyas ring:
God's highest glory was their anthem still,
Peace on the earth, and mutual goodwill.

John Byrom (1692–1763)

*Byrom's little daughter,
Dolly, asked him to write
her a poem as a
Christmas present. On
Christmas morning 1749
she found on her plate
these lines on a sheet of
paper headed 'Christmas
Day. For Dolly.' The
following Christmas the
Byroms were woken up by
the choir of Stockport
parish church singing
'Christians awake!'
beneath their windows, to
the tune 'Yorkshire' that
John Wainwright*

4 To Bethl'em straight th'enlightened shepherds run
  To see the wonder that the Lord has done,
  And find, with Joseph and the blessèd Maid,
  Her Son, the Saviour, in a manger laid;
  Then to their flocks, still praising God, return,
  And their glad hearts with holy rapture burn.

5 O may we keep and ponder in our mind
  God's wondrous love in saving humankind;
  Trace we the Babe, who hath retrieved our loss,
  From his poor manger to his bitter cross;
  Tread in his steps, assisted by his grace,
  Till our first heavenly state again takes place.

6 Then may we hope, th'angelic hosts among,
  To sing, redeemed, a glad triumphal song.
  He that was born upon this joyful day
  Around us all his glory shall display;
  Saved by his love, incessant we shall sing
  Eternal praise to heav'n's almighty King.

*(1723–68), their local
church organist, had
especially composed for it.*

---

16 *Come, come, come to the manger*

Come, come, come to the manger,
Children, come to the children's King;
Sing, sing, chorus of angels,
Stars of morning, o'er Bethlehem sing!

1 He lies 'mid the beasts of the stall,
  Who is Maker and Lord of us all;
  The wintry wind blows cold and dreary,
  See, he weeps, the world is weary,
  Lord, have pity and mercy on me.

    Come, come, come to the manger, . . .

2 To the manger of Bethlehem come,
  To the Saviour Emmanuel's home;
  The heavenly hosts above are singing,
  Set the Christmas bells a-ringing,
  Lord, have pity and mercy on me.

    Come, come, come to the manger, . . .

*John Robert, Abbot of
Downside*

*Words © John Robert.
Used by kind permission.*

*A 'wintry wind' blows
through this children's
carol, which returns,
nevertheless, to a joyful
refrain.
    The lively traditional
tune lends itself to simple
accompaniment on
recorders or percussion.*

17 Come, they told me
(The Little Drummer)

1 Come, they told me, parum pum pum pum,
   A new-born king to see, parum pum pum pum,
   Our finest gifts we bring, parum pum pum pum,
   To lay before the king, parum pum pum pum,
   Rum pum pum pum, rum pum pum pum.
   So to honour him, parum pum pum pum,
   When we come.

2 Baby Jesus, parum pum pum pum,
   I am a poor child too, parum pum pum pum,
   I have no gift to bring, parum pum pum pum,
   That's fit to give our king, parum pum pum pum,
   Rum pum pum pum, rum pum pum pum.
   Shall I play for you, parum pum pum pum,
   On my drum?

3 Mary nodded, parum pum pum pum,
   The ox and ass kept time, parum pum pum pum,
   I played my drum for him, parum pum pum pum,
   I played my best for him, parum pum pum pum,
   Rum pum pum pum, rum pum pum pum.
   Then he smiled at me, parum pum pum pum,
   Me and my drum.

Katherine K. Davis, Harry Simeone and Henry Onorati

Words and music © 1958 Mills Music Inc., USA, and International Music Corp., USA; Chappell Music Ltd, London W1Y 3FA

The Christmas story seen through the eyes of a poor child, who visits the manger and, having no other gift, plays the drum for Jesus and Mary. It has been recorded by many famous names in the pop music world.
The tune is a traditional Czech carol melody

---

18 Come, thou long-expected Jesus

1 Come, thou long-expected Jesus,
   Born to set thy people free,
   From our fears and sins release us,
   Let us find our rest in thee.

2 Israel's strength and consolation,
   Hope of all the earth thou art,
   Dear desire of every nation,
   Joy of every longing heart.

3 Born thy people to deliver,
   Born a child and yet a king,
   Born to reign in us for ever,
   Now thy gracious kingdom bring.

4 By thine own eternal spirit,
   Rule in all our hearts alone;
   By thine all-sufficient merit
   Raise us to thy glorious throne.

Charles Wesley (1707–88)

A hymn that emphasizes the kingship of Jesus, this first appeared in Charles Wesley's Hymns for the Nativity of our Lord (1744) in two eight-line verses.
It is now usually sung, as here, to the fine four-line tune 'Cross of Jesus', by John Stainer (1840–1901).

---

19 *Dans cette étable*

1 Dans cette étable
   Que Jésus est charmant,
   Qu'il est aimable
   Dans son abaissement!
   Que d'attraits à la fois!
   Tous les palais des rois
   N'ont rien de comparable
   Aux beautés que je vois dans cette étable!

2 Plus de misère!
   Un Dieu souffre pour nous,
   Et de son Père
   Désarme le courroux;
   C'est en notre faveur
   Qu'il est dans la douleur.
   Pouvait-il pour nous plaire
   Unir à sa grandeur plus de misère?

3 Que sa puissance
   Reluit bien en ce jour!
   Malgré l'enfance
   Où le reduit l'amour.
   Notre ennemi dompté,
   L'enfer déconcerté,
   Font voir qu'à sa naissance
   Rien n'est plus redouté que sa puissance!

Fléchier (1632–1710)

No translation is quite satisfactory or necessary for this simply worded traditional French carol. It expresses the appeal of Jesus' humble birth in a poor stable, in contrast with the empty trappings of earthly power, and compares the love and sweetness of the child, born into poverty and suffering, to the acts of love and suffering that he will later endure in his life and death.

   It is sometimes called 'Gounod's Bethlehem' because the traditional tune was arranged by Charles Gounod (1818–93).

---

20 *Deck the hall with boughs of holly*

1 Deck the hall with boughs of holly,
      Fa la la la la, la la la la.
   'Tis the season to be jolly,
      Fa la la la la, la la la la.
   Don we now our gay apparel,
      Fa la la, la la la, la la la.
   Troll the ancient Yuletide carol,
      Fa la la la la, la la la la.

2 See the blazing Yule before us,
      Fa la la la la, la la la la.
   Strike the harp and join the chorus,
      Fa la la la la, la la la la.
   Follow me in merry measure,
      Fa la la, la la la, la la la.
   While I tell of Yuletide treasure,
      Fa la la la la, la la la la.

Welsh traditional

A secular carol, long popular with carol singers out on cold winter nights. Also suitable for New Year services.

   'Nos Galan' is a traditional Welsh tune, arranged here by John Barnard.

3 Fast away the old year passes,
  Fa la la la la, la la la la.
Hail the new, ye lads and lasses,
  Fa la la la la, la la la la.
Sing we joyous all together,
  Fa la la, la la, la la la la.
Heedless of the wind and weather,
  Fa la la la la, la la la la.

---

21 *Deep peace of the running wave to you (A Gaelic Blessing)*

Deep peace of the running wave to you,
Deep peace of the flowing air to you,
Deep peace of the quiet earth to you,
Deep peace of the shining stars to you,
Deep peace of the gentle night to you,
Moon and stars pour their healing light on you,
Deep peace of Christ,
Of Christ the light of the world to you,
Deep peace of Christ to you.

Ancient Gaelic blessing, adapted John Rutter (b. 1945)

Words and musical arrangement © John Rutter. Used by permission of the Royal School of Church Music.

John Rutter's setting of an ancient Gaelic blessing, which was commissioned by a Methodist church in the USA for Mel Olson, has become popular with non-choral singers, mainly through being sung on BBC TV's Songs of Praise. John Rutter has made a simplified arrangement especially for this collection, so that all carol singers can attempt this beautiful piece, which is ideal for ending a carol service.

---

22 *Ding-dong, ding, ding-a-dong-a-ding (Up, good Christen folk)*

Ding-dong, ding, ding-a-dong-a-ding:
Ding-dong, ding-dong, ding-a-dong-ding.

1 Up! good Christen folk, and listen
How the merry church bells ring.
And from steeple bid good people
Come adore the new-born King:

George Ratcliffe Woodward (1848–1934)

As in 'Ding dong! merrily on high' (no. 23), Woodward wants carol singers to imitate the

2 Tell the story how from glory
   God came down at Christmas-tide,
   Bringing gladness, chasing sadness,
   Show'ring blessings far and wide.

3 Born of mother, blest o'er other,
   Ex Maria Virgine,
   In a stable ('tis no fable),
   Christus natus hodie.

   Ding-dong, ding, ding-a-dong-a-ding:
   Ding-dong, ding-dong, ding-a-dong-ding.

*sound of the Christmas
church bells.*

   The melody is from Piae
Cantiones *(1582).*

---

23 *Ding dong! merrily on high*

1 Ding dong! merrily on high
   In heav'n the bells are ringing:
   Ding dong! verily the sky
   Is riv'n with angel-singing.

   Gloria! Hosanna in excelsis!
   Gloria! Hosanna in excelsis!

2 E'en so here below, below,
   Let steeple bells be swungen,
   And i-o, i-o, i-o,
   By priest and people sungen.

   Gloria! Hosanna in excelsis! . . .

3 Pray you, dutifully prime
   Your matin chime, ye ringers;
   May you beautifully rime
   Your evetime song, ye singers.

   Gloria! Hosanna in excelsis! . . .

*George Ratcliffe
Woodward (1848–1934)*

*A carol, to a 16th-century
French tune, that imitates
and praises the sound of
Christmas church bells. It
needs plenty of bounce in
performance.*

   *'I-o' should be
pronounced 'ee-o'.*

---

24 *Every star shall sing a carol*

1 Every star shall sing a carol;
   Every creature, high or low,
   Come and praise the King of Heaven
   By whatever name you know.

   God above, Man below,
   Holy is the name I know.

Sydney Carter (b. 1915)

2 When the King of all creation
  Had a cradle on the earth,
  Holy was the human body,
  Holy was the human birth.

    God above, Man below, . . .

3 Who can tell what other cradle
  High above the Milky Way
  Still may rock the King of Heaven
  On another Christmas Day?

    God above, Man below, . . .

4 Who can count how many crosses
  Still to come or long ago
  Crucify the King of Heaven?
  Holy is the name I know.

    God above, Man below, . . .

5 Who can tell what other body
  He will hallow for his own?
  I will praise the Son of Mary,
  Brother of my blood and bone.

    God above, Man below, . . .

6 Every star and every planet,
  Every creature high and low,
  Come and praise the King of Heaven
  By whatever name you know.

    God above, Man below, . . .

*USA © 1961, Galliard Ltd.
Used by permission of
Galaxy Music Corp.,
Boston.*

*'By whatever name you
know.' Anyone with a
sense of the numinous,
but lacking in certainty or
desire to possess a fixed set
of truths, will like Sydney
Carter's words, born out
of doubt, bright with
hope. He says 'Song, God,
a waving possibility: you
must trust it, travel with it
— or it is not there'.*

---

25 Girls and boys, leave your toys, make no noise (Zither Carol)

1 Girls and boys, leave your toys, make no noise,
  Kneel at his crib and worship him.
  At thy shrine, Child divine, we are thine,
  Our Saviour's here.

    'Hallelujah' the church bells ring,
    'Hallelujah' the angels sing,
    'Hallelujah' from everything.
    All must draw near.

2 On that day, far away, Jesus lay,
  Angels were watching round his head.
  Holy child, mother mild, undefiled,
  We sing thy praise.

    'Hallelujah' the church bells ring, . . .

*Malcolm Sargent
(1895–1967)*

*Words and music used by
permission of Oxford
University Press.*

*Words by Sir Malcolm
Sargent, who helped so
many to enjoy music and
to love singing. Children
are called to leave their
toys and games, and
come and worship at the
manger with the
shepherds and angels.*

3 Shepherds came at the fame of thy name,
Angels their guide to Bethlehem.
In that place, saw thy face filled with grace,
Stood at thy door.

  'Hallelujah' the church bells ring, . . .

*Always known as the
'Zither Carol'; the tune is
a traditional Czech folk
dance.*

26 *Gloria, gloria, in excelsis Deo*

Gloria, gloria, in excelsis Deo,
Gloria, gloria, alleluia!
Et in terra pax hominibus
Bonae voluntatis.

Jacques Berthier

*Words and music ©
Ateliers et Presses de
Taizé, 71250 Taizé
Communauté, France.
Used by permission.*

*A canon from Taizé, an
ecumenical Christian
community in Burgundy,
France, which today
attracts huge numbers of
pilgrims, particularly
young people, from all
around the world. This
'Gloria' has become very
popular with the pilgrims,
and is sung, as part of the
Christmas liturgy, in
four-part canon.*

27 *God rest ye merry, gentlemen*

1 God rest ye merry, gentlemen,
Let nothing you dismay,
Remember Christ our Saviour
Was born on Christmas Day,
To save us all from Satan's power
When we were gone astray:

  O tidings of comfort and joy,
  Comfort and joy!
  O tidings of comfort and joy!

English traditional

*A popular traditional
carol, harmonized by
John Stainer
(1840–1901). Frequently
heard on the streets of
London in the 18th and
19th centuries, this
version of St Luke's*

2 From God our heavenly Father
   A blessèd angel came,
   And unto certain shepherds
   Brought tidings of the same,
   How that in Bethlehem was born
   The son of God by name:

   O tidings of comfort and joy, . . .

3 And when they came to Bethlehem
   Where our dear Saviour lay,
   They found him in a manger,
   Where oxen feed on hay;
   His mother Mary kneeling down,
   Unto the Lord did pray:

   O tidings of comfort and joy, . . .

4 Now to the Lord sing praises,
   All you within this place,
   And with true love and fellowship
   Each other now embrace;
   This holy tide of Christmas
   All other doth efface:

   O tidings of comfort and joy, . . .

Christmas story has the purpose of drawing everyone (not only gentlemen!) into the experience of the shepherds. The first four words are, of course, a greeting, so the placing of the comma is important.

---

28 *Good King Wenceslas looked out*

1 Good King Wenceslas looked out
   On the Feast of Stephen,
   When the snow lay round about,
   Deep, and crisp, and even:
   Brightly shone the moon that night,
   Though the frost was cruel,
   When a poor man came in sight
   Gath'ring winter fuel.

2 'Hither, page, and stand by me,
   If thou know'st it, telling.
   Yonder peasant, who is he?
   Where and what his dwelling?'
   'Sire, he lives a good league hence,
   Underneath the mountain,
   Right against the forest fence,
   By Saint Agnes' fountain.'

*John Mason Neale
(1818–66)*

A carol that tells an imaginary story based on a real person. The Feast of Stephen is the day after Christmas, i.e. Boxing Day; Wenceslas (c. 907– 929), prince and martyr, became the patron saint of Bohemia and the symbol of Czech independence.

3 'Bring me flesh, and bring me wine,
  Bring me pine logs hither:
  Thou and I will see him dine,
  When we bear them thither.'
  Page and monarch, forth they went,
  Forth they went together;
  Through the rude wind's wild lament
  And the bitter weather.

4 'Sire, the night is darker now,
  And the wind blows stronger;
  Fails my heart, I know not how;
  I can go no longer.'
  'Mark my footsteps, good my page;
  Tread thou in them boldly:
  Thou shalt find the winter's rage
  Freeze thy blood less coldly.'

5 In his master's steps he trod,
  Where the snow lay dinted;
  Heat was in the very sod
  Which the Saint had printed.
  Therefore, Christians all, be sure,
  Wealth or rank possessing,
  Ye who now will bless the poor,
  Shall yourselves find blessing.

---

29 *Go, tell it on the mountain*

American traditional

> Go, tell it on the mountain,
> Over the hills and everywhere
> Go, tell it on the mountain
> That Jesus Christ is born!

1 While shepherds sat a-watching
  Their silent flocks by night,
  There shone throughout the heavens
  A great and glorious light.

> Go, tell it on the mountain, . . .

2 The shepherds feared and trembled
  When, high above the earth,
  Rang out the angel chorus
  That hailed our Saviour's birth.

> Go, tell it on the mountain, . . .

---

30   *Hail, Mary, full of grace*

1 Hail, Mary, full of grace,
   You are blessed, the Lord is with you.
   Through his angel God is asking
   You to be the mother of his son.
   Speak, Mary, for us all:
   There's no sweeter music heard
   Than your gladly whispered answer
   'Let it be to me according to your word.'

2 Good news for humankind;
   Joseph hears the joyful message:
   God will come to us in Jesus,
   'He will save his people from their sins'.
   Jesus, Emmanuel,
   May my wayward will be stirred
   Day by day to pray with Mary:
   'Let it be to me according to your word.'

Patrick Appleford
(b. 1925)

Words and music ©
Patrick Appleford 1990.
Used by kind permission.

*A new carol with a 'gladly
whispered' prayer in each
verse. It remembers that
Joseph, too, shared in the
extraordinary experience
of being visited by angels.*

---

31   *Hail to the Lord's Anointed!*

1 Hail to the Lord's Anointed!
   Great David's greater Son;
   Hail, in the time appointed,
   His reign on earth begun!
   He comes to break oppression,
   To set the captive free;
   To take away transgression,
   And rule in equity.

2 He comes with succour speedy
   To those who suffer wrong;
   To help the poor and needy,
   And bid the weak be strong;
   To give them songs for sighing,
   Their darkness turn to light,
   Whose souls, condemned and dying,
   Were precious in his sight.

3 He shall come down like showers
   Upon the fruitful earth,
   And love, joy, hope, like flowers,
   Spring in his path to birth:
   Before him on the mountains
   Shall peace the herald go;
   And righteousness in fountains
   From hill to valley flow.

James Montgomery
(1771–1854)

*A free paraphrase of
Psalm 72, and a strong,
missionary hymn, by one
of the foremost social
reformers of his day.*
   *'Crüger' is an
adaptation by W. H.
Monk (1823–89), in
1861, of a 17th-century
chorale by Johann Crüger
(1598–1662). It needs to
be sung with passion and
dignity.*

4 Kings shall fall down before him,
   And gold and incense bring;
   All nations shall adore him,
   His praise all people sing;
   To him shall prayer unceasing
   And daily vows ascend;
   His kingdom still increasing,
   A kingdom without end.

5 O'er every foe victorious,
   He on his throne shall rest,
   From age to age more glorious,
   All-blessing and all-blest:
   The tide of time shall never
   His covenant remove;
   His name shall stand for ever;
   That name to us is Love.

32 *Hark! A herald voice is calling*

1 Hark! a herald voice is calling:
   'Christ is nigh', it seems to say;
   'Cast away the dreams of darkness,
   O ye children of the day!'

2 Startled at the solemn warning,
   Let the earth-bound soul arise;
   Christ, her Sun, all sloth dispelling,
   Shines upon the morning skies.

3 Lo! the Lamb, so long expected,
   Comes with pardon down from Heaven;
   Let us haste, with tears of sorrow,
   One and all to be forgiven;

4 So when next he comes in glory,
   And earth's final hour draws near,
   May he then as our defender
   On the clouds of heaven appear.

5 Honour, glory, virtue, merit,
   To the Father and the Son,
   With the co-eternal Spirit,
   While unending ages run.

*Latin, 6th century,
tr. Edward Caswall
(1814–78), amended*

*Based on Romans 13.11
and Luke 21.25–27, this
was the Lauds hymn
during Advent in the
Sarum and other ancient
prayer books. The words
have been extensively
altered by different editors
over the years, and we
hope this version brings
out the truth for people of
today.*

   *The tune, 'Merton', is by
W. H. Monk (1823–89).*

33 Hark the glad sound! the Saviour comes

1 Hark the glad sound! the Saviour comes,
  The Saviour promised long!
  Let every heart prepare a throne,
  And every voice a song.

2 He comes the prisoners to release
  In Satan's bondage held;
  The gates of brass before him burst,
  The iron fetters yield.

3 He comes the broken heart to bind,
  The bleeding soul to cure,
  And with the treasures of his grace
  Enrich the humble poor.

4 Our glad hosannas, Prince of Peace,
  Thy welcome shall proclaim,
  And heaven's eternal arches ring
  With thy belovèd name.

Philip Doddridge
(1702–51)

The original manuscript, published in 1735, is headed 'Christ's Message, from Luke 4.18, 19' (where Jesus read Isaiah 61.1, 2). Like many of Doddridge's hymns, this was designed to be sung immediately after he had preached on the text.
'Bristol' comes from Ravenscroft's Psalter *(1621).*

---

34 Hark! the herald angels sing

1 Hark! the herald angels sing
  Glory to the new-born King;
  Peace on earth and mercy mild,
  God and sinners reconciled:
  Joyful all ye nations rise,
  Join the triumph of the skies,
  With the angelic host proclaim,
  Christ is born in Bethlehem.

    Hark! the herald angels sing
    Glory to the new-born King.

2 Christ, by highest heaven adored,
  Christ, the everlasting Lord,
  Late in time behold him come
  Offspring of a Virgin's womb!
  Veiled in flesh the Godhead see,
  Hail the incarnate Deity!
  Pleased as man with man to dwell,
  Jesus, our Emmanuel:

    Hark! the herald angels sing . . .

Charles Wesley (1707–88), G. Whitefield (in 1753), M. Madan (in 1760) and others

Probably the best-known carol in the world. Charles Wesley's original 1743 carol ('Hark how all the welkin ring') was and is very fine in its own right, but alterations made by Whitefield and others have made it universally acclaimed.
'Mendelssohn' is an adaptation by Dr William Hayman Cummings of a chorus in Mendelssohn's secular cantata Festgesang. *The composer himself, however,*

3 Hail the heaven-born Prince of Peace!
  Hail the Sun of Righteousness!
  Light and life to all he brings,
  Risen with healing in his wings;
  Mild he lays his glory by,
  Born that man no more may die,
  Born to raise the sons of earth,
  Born to give them second birth:

    Hark! the herald angels sing . . .

*considered the tune
unsuitable for sacred
words, describing it in a
letter to his publisher as
'soldierlike and buxom'!*

*The last two lines and
the refrain sometimes
stretch the capacity of
many singers, so we have
transposed the tune down;
you should also notice that
the last two lines of the
verse have the same notes
as the refrain, but a
slightly different rhythm.*

---

35 *Here we go up to Bethlehem*

1 Here we go up to Bethlehem,
  Bethlehem, Bethlehem,
  Here we go up to Bethlehem
  On a cold and frosty morning.

2 We've got to be taxed in Bethlehem,
  Bethlehem, Bethlehem,
  We've got to be taxed in Bethlehem
  On a cold and frosty morning.

3 Where shall we stay in Bethlehem,
  Bethlehem, Bethlehem?
  Where shall we stay in Bethlehem
  On a cold and frosty morning?

Sydney Carter (b. 1915)

*Words © Sydney Carter.
Used by permission of
Stainer & Bell.
USA © 1965, Galliard Ltd.
Used by permission of
Galaxy Music Corp.,
Boston.*

*New words to the
traditional English
melody for 'Here we go
round the mulberry bush!'
Written for children, and
it's a good idea to ask
them to make up extra
verses to finish the story,
which is deliberately left
incomplete.*

---

36 *He smiles within his cradle*

1 He smiles within his cradle,
  A babe with face so bright
  It beams most like a mirror
  Against a blaze of light:
  This babe so burning bright.

*Austrian, tr. Robert
Graves*

*Words © Robert Graves,
from the* Oxford Book of
Carols. *Reprinted by*

24

2 This babe we now declare to you
  Is Jesus Christ our Lord;
  He brings both peace and heartiness:
  Haste, haste with one accord
  To feast with Christ our Lord.

3 And who would rock the cradle
  Wherein this infant lies,
  Must rock with easy motion
  And watch with humble eyes,
  Like Mary pure and wise.

4 O Jesus, dearest babe of all
  And dearest babe of mine,
  Thy love is great, thy limbs are small.
  O, flood this heart of mine
  With overflow from thine!

permission of Oxford
University Press.

The Austrian words and
tune 'Ein Kindlein in der
Wiegen' first appeared in
Vienna in 1649 in D. G.
Corner's Geistliche
Nachtigall. *Robert*
Graves's 1928 translation
has made this gentle
lullaby carol very popular
in Britain, too.

---

37 *Hills of the North, rejoice*

1 Hills of the North, rejoice,
  Echoing songs arise,
  Hail with united voice
  Him who made earth and skies:
  He comes in righteousness and love,
  He brings salvation from above.

2 Isles of the southern seas,
  Sing to the listening earth,
  Carry on every breeze
  Hope of a world's new birth:
  In Christ shall all be made anew,
  His word is sure, his promise true.

3 Lands of the East, arise,
  He is your brightest morn,
  Greet him with joyous eyes,
  Praise shall his path adorn:
  The God whom you have longed to know
  In Christ draws near, and calls you now.

4 Shores of the utmost West,
  Lands of the setting sun,
  Welcome the heavenly guest
  In whom the dawn has come:
  He brings a never-ending light
  Who triumphed o'er our darkest night.

Based on words by
Charles E. Oakley
(1832– 65)

Words (this version) used
by permission of Oxford
University Press.

A stirring missionary
hymn, suitable for both
Advent and Epiphany. It
is the one relic of a short
and brilliant life,
although Oakley's
original words have had
to be extensively revised.
*   Martin Shaw (1875–*
1958) composed 'Little
Cornard' especially for
this hymn, and the
change of rhythm in the
last two lines adds great
power.

5 Shout, as you journey on,
  Songs be in every mouth,
  Lo, from the North they come,
  From East and West and South:
  In Jesus all shall find their rest,
  In him shall all the earth be blest.

---

38 *Holy Child, how still you lie*

1 Holy Child, how still you lie!
  Safe the manger, soft the hay;
  Faint upon the eastern sky
  Breaks the dawn of Christmas Day.

2 Holy Child, whose birthday brings
  Shepherds from their field and fold,
  Angel choirs and eastern kings,
  Myrrh and frankincense and gold:

3 Holy Child, what gift of grace
  From the Father freely willed!
  In your infant form we trace
  All God's promises fulfilled.

4 Holy Child, whose human years
  Span like ours delight and pain;
  One in human joys and tears,
  One in all but sin and stain:

5 Holy Child, so far from home,
  All the lost to seek and save,
  To what dreadful death you come,
  To what dark and silent grave!

6 Holy Child, before whose name
  Powers of darkness faint and fall;
  Conquered, death and sin and shame —
  Jesus Christ is Lord of all!

7 Holy Child, how still you lie!
  Safe the manger, soft the hay;
  Clear upon the eastern sky
  Breaks the dawn of Christmas Day.

Timothy Dudley-Smith (b. 1926)

A quiet song addressed to Jesus in the manger, meditating on the mysterious way that all the promises surrounding his birth on Christmas morning will be fulfilled.

Michael Baughen's tune 'Holy Child' has a different melody for alternate verses.

39 How brightly shines the Morning Star!

1 How brightly shines the Morning Star!
The nations see and hail afar
The Light in Judah shining.
Thou David's son of Jacob's race,
The Bridegroom, and the King of Grace,
For thee our hearts are pining!
Lowly, holy,
Great and glorious, thou victorious
Prince of Graces,
Filling all the heavenly places!

2 Though circled by the hosts on high,
He deigns to cast a pitying eye
Upon his helpless creature;
The whole creation's Head and Lord,
By highest seraphim adored,
Assumes our very nature.
Jesu, grant us,
Through thy merit, to inherit
Thy salvation;
Hear, O hear our supplication.

3 Rejoice, ye heav'ns; thou earth, reply;
With praise, ye sinners, fill the sky,
For this his Incarnation.
Incarnate God, put forth thy power,
Ride on, ride on, great Conqueror,
Till all know thy salvation.
Amen, Amen!
Alleluya, Alleluya!
Praise be given
Evermore by earth and heaven.

Philipp Nicolai (1556–1608), tr. William Mercer (1811–73)

The German words, and probably the tune, were composed by Nicolai in 1599, during the same terrible pestilence as 'Wake! O Wake!' (no. 108).

Much of the popularity of this hymn is due to the tune, a famous chorale, 'Wie Schön Leuchtet der Morgenstern', that was soon set on many city chimes in Germany. This arrangement is by Felix Mendelssohn (1809–47), from his oratorio Christus.

40 How lovely on the mountains are the feet of him (Our God Reigns)

1 How lovely on the mountains are the feet of him
Who brings good news, good news,
Proclaiming peace, announcing news of happiness:
Our God reigns, our God reigns!

Our God reigns, our God reigns,
Our God reigns, our God reigns!

Leonard E. Smith Jr

Words and music © 1974, 1978 New Jerusalem Music. Used by permission of Thankyou Music.

2 You watchmen lift your voices joyfully as one,
  Shout for your king, your king;
  See eye to eye the Lord restoring Zion:
  Your God reigns, your God reigns!

      Your God reigns, your God reigns, . . .

3 Waste places of Jerusalem, break forth with joy —
  We are redeemed, redeemed;
  The Lord has saved and comforted his people:
  Your God reigns, your God reigns!

      Your God reigns, your God reigns, . . .

4 Ends of the earth, see the salvation of your God —
  Jesus is Lord, is Lord!
  Before the nations he has bared his holy arm:
  Your God reigns, your God reigns!

      Your God reigns, your God reigns, . . .

Based on Isaiah 52, this rapidly became popular and has been heard at great gatherings, from the crowds at the open-air Masses during Pope John Paul II's visit to Britain in 1982, to Greenbelt festivals and Spring Harvest gatherings.

---

41 *Il est né le divin enfant*

  Il est né le divin enfant
  Jouez hautbois, résonnez musettes;
  Il est né le divin enfant
  Chantons tous son avènement.

1 Ah! qu'il est beau, qu'il est charmant!
  Ah! que ses grâces sont parfaites!
  Ah! qu'il est beau, qu'il est charmant!
  Qu'il est doux ce divin enfant.

      Il est né le divin enfant . . .

2 Une étable est son logement,
  Un peu de paille est sa couchette;
  Une étable est son logement
  Pour un Dieu quel abaissement!

      Il est né le divin enfant . . .

3 Partez grands rois de l'Orient,
  Venez vous unir à nos fêtes!
  Partez grands rois de l'Orient,
  Venez adorer cet enfant.

      Il est né le divin enfant . . .

French traditional

This French carol involves the instruments in a canticle of praise. A musette is a kind of aristocratic bagpipe, and also a smooth and simple pastoral dance. As you sing, imagine a droning accompaniment . . .

---

42 I'm standing at windows, and knocking on doors (Georgie)

I'm standing at windows,
And knocking on doors,
I'm not sure of my welcome,
I'm too tattered and torn,
When shoppers walk round me,
I smile and I say,
'Give a penny to Georgie for Christmas Day.'
For Christmas Day, for Christmas Day,
Give a penny to Georgie for Christmas Day.

Sarah Mason

*Words and music ©
Sarah Mason. Used by
kind permission.*

*This was first performed
in 1984, at the Inner
London Education
Authority's annual
Festival of Carols: the
author of both words and
music was at the time a
pupil at the Grey Coat
Hospital School. Like 'The
Little Drummer', Georgie
is poor, but he is stuck in
the streets of a modern
city surrounded by
uncaring shoppers.*
  *It might be best to sing
this through twice: each
time, repeat the last two
lines, but humming
instead of singing the
words.*

43 In a byre near Bethlehem (The Word of Life)

1 In a byre near Bethlehem,
   Passed by many a wand'ring stranger,
   The most precious Word of Life
   Was heard gurgling in a manger,
   For the good of us all.

      And he's here when we call him,
      Bringing health, love and laughter
      To life now and ever after,
      For the good of us all.

2 By the Galilean Lake
   Where the people flocked for teaching,
   The most precious Word of Life
   Fed their mouths as well as preaching,
   For the good of us all.

      And he's here when we call him, . . .

Scottish traditional

*Words and musical
arrangement © 1987
Iona Community/Wild
Goose Publications,
Pearce Institute, Govan,
Glasgow G51 3UT,
Scotland (from* Heaven
Shall Not Wait*). Used by
permission.*

*Gaelic prayers are always
rich in gospel images and
phrases, and this hymn
from the Iona Community
echoes a phrase from the
great meditation opening*

3 Quiet was Gethsemane,
  Camouflaging priest and soldier;
  The most precious Word of Life
  Took the world's weight on his shoulder,
  For the good of us all.

    And he's here when we call him, . . .

4 On the hill of Calvary —
  Place to end all hope of living —
  The most precious Word of Life
  Breathed his last and died, forgiving,
  For the good of us all.

    And he's here when we call him, . . .

5 In a garden, just at dawn,
  Near the grave of human violence,
  The most precious Word of Life
  Cleared his throat and ended silence,
  For the good of us all.

    And he's here when we call him, . . .

St John's gospel: 'In the beginning was the Word, and the Word was with God, and the Word was God . . .'. The hymn tells the story of Jesus, from his birth to his death and resurrection, assuring us that the Word of Life is still here for us all.

---

44 *In dulci jubilo*

1 In dulci jubilo
  Now sing we all i-o, i-o,
  He, our love, our pleasure
  Lies in praesepio,
  Like brightly gleaming treasure
  Matris in gremio:
  Alpha es et O!
  Alpha es et O!

2 O Jesu parvule,
  For you I long alway;
  Hear me in my sadness,
  O puer optime;
  With goodness and with gladness,
  O princeps gloriae,
  Trahe me post te!
  Trahe me post te!

3 O Patris caritas!
  O Nati lenitas!
  We were past reprieving
  Per nostra crimina;
  For us you are retrieving
  Coelorum gaudia,
  O that we were there!
  O that we were there!

German/Latin, 14th century, tr. Geoffrey Court

Being half in Latin and half (originally) in German, this carol is known as 'macaronic' — we suppose a mediaeval form of 'Franglais'. The original words are said to have been sung by angels to Henry Suso, the mystic, who then danced with his celestial visitors (who, incidentally, pronounced 'i-o' as 'ee-o'). This is a new translation by Geoffrey Court.

The original melody is also 14th-century. It was harmonized by Robert Lucas de Pearsall (1795–1856) and arranged here by W. J. Westbrook.

4 Ubi sunt gaudia?
  O nowhere more than there;
  Angels there are singing
  Nova cantica,
  And there the bells are ringing
  In regis curia,
  O that we were there!
  O that we were there!

---

45 *Infant holy, infant lowly*

1 Infant holy, infant lowly,
  For his bed a cattle stall;
  Oxen lowing, little knowing
  Christ the babe is Lord of all.
  Swift are winging, angels singing,
  Nowells ringing, tidings bringing,
  Christ the babe is Lord of all,
  Christ the babe is Lord of all.

2 Flocks were sleeping, shepherds keeping
  Vigil till the morning new;
  Saw the glory, heard the story,
  Tidings of a gospel true.
  Thus rejoicing, free from sorrow,
  Praises voicing, greet the morrow,
  Christ the babe was born for you!
  Christ the babe was born for you!

Polish, tr. Edith M. Reed

This English version of a Polish carol was made in the mid-1920s by Miss Reed for Music and Youth, *and became very popular in schools.*

Little is known about the origin of the tune, although it is probably also traditional Polish.

---

46 *In the bleak midwinter*

1 In the bleak midwinter
  Frosty wind made moan,
  Earth stood hard as iron,
  Water like a stone:
  Snow had fallen, snow on snow,
  Snow on snow,
  In the bleak midwinter,
  Long ago.

2 Our God, heaven cannot hold him
  Nor earth sustain;
  Heaven and earth shall flee away
  When he comes to reign:
  In the bleak midwinter
  A stable place sufficed
  The Lord God Almighty,
  Jesus Christ.

*Christina Rossetti
(1830–94)*

The beautiful words are matched by Gustav Holst's simple, heart-catching tune 'Cranham'.

At first sight, the words can be difficult to fit in, especially at the beginnings of lines. It helps to notice which are the important syllables, and put those on the strong beats (in verse 2, for example, 'God', 'stable', 'Lord').

3 Enough for him, whom Cherubim
   Worship night and day,
   A breastful of milk,
   And a manger full of hay:
   Enough for him, whom angels
   Fall down before,
   The ox and ass and camel
   Which adore.

4 Angels and archangels
   May have gathered there,
   Cherubim and seraphim
   Thronged the air
   But only his mother
   In her maiden bliss
   Worshipped the Belovèd
   With a kiss.

5 What can I give him,
   Poor as I am?
   If I were a shepherd
   I would bring a lamb;
   If I were a wise man
   I would do my part;
   Yet what I can I give him:
   Give my heart.

---

47 *I saw three ships come sailing in*

1 I saw three ships come sailing in,
   On Christmas Day, on Christmas Day,
   I saw three ships come sailing in,
   On Christmas Day in the morning.

2 And what was in those ships all three,
   On Christmas Day, on Christmas Day,
   And what was in those ships all three,
   On Christmas Day in the morning?

3 Our Saviour Christ and his Ladie,
   On Christmas Day, on Christmas Day,
   Our Saviour Christ and his Ladie,
   On Christmas Day in the morning.

4 Pray, whither sailed those ships all three,
   On Christmas Day, on Christmas Day,
   Pray, whither sailed those ships all three,
   On Christmas Day in the morning?

5 O they sailed into Bethlehem,
   On Christmas Day, on Christmas Day,
   O they sailed into Bethlehem,
   On Christmas Day in the morning.

English traditional

Another traditional folk carol that was sung all over Victorian England, sometimes in a version which begins 'As I sat on a sunny bank'. It tells a legendary story for Christmas through question and answer, and works well when the singers divide to sing alternate verses.

6 And all the bells on earth shall ring,
   On Christmas Day, on Christmas Day,
   And all the bells on earth shall ring,
   On Christmas Day in the morning.

7 And all the angels in heaven shall sing,
   On Christmas Day, on Christmas Day,
   And all the angels in heaven shall sing,
   On Christmas Day in the morning.

8 And all the souls on earth shall sing,
   On Christmas Day, on Christmas Day,
   And all the souls on earth shall sing,
   On Christmas Day in the morning.

9 Then let us all rejoice amain,
   On Christmas Day, on Christmas Day,
   Then let us all rejoice amain,
   On Christmas Day in the morning.

---

48 *It came upon the midnight clear*

1 It came upon the midnight clear,
   That glorious song of old,
   From angels bending near the earth
   To touch their harps of gold:
   'Peace on the earth, good-will to men,
   From heaven's all gracious King!'
   The world in solemn stillness lay
   To hear the angels sing.

2 Still through the cloven skies they come,
   With peaceful wings unfurled;
   And still their heavenly music floats
   O'er all the weary world;
   Above its sad and lowly plains
   They bend on hovering wing;
   And ever o'er its Babel sounds
   The blessèd angels sing.

3 Yet with the woes of sin and strife
   The world has suffered long;
   Beneath the angel-strain have rolled
   Two thousand years of wrong;
   And man, at war with man, hears not
   The love-song which they bring:
   O hush the noise, ye men of strife,
   And hear the angels sing!

Edmund Sears (1810–76)

One of the few Victorian carols to emphasize the social message of Christmas: Peace on earth. It was written by an American Unitarian minister, and its powerful plea for peace came, ironically, just ten years before the American Civil War broke out.

The tune, 'Noël', is by Arthur Sullivan (1842–1900).

4 For lo! the days are hastening on,
  By prophet bards foretold,
  When, with the ever-circling years,
  Comes round the age of gold;
  When peace shall over all the earth
  Its ancient splendours fling,
  And the whole world give back the song
  Which now the angels sing.

---

49 *It was on a starry night*
      (A Starry Night)

1 It was on a starry night
  When the hills were bright,
  Earth lay sleeping, sleeping calm and still.
  Then in a cattle shed
  In a manger bed,
  A child was born King of all the world.

  And all the angels sang for him,
  The bells of heaven rang for him,
  For a child was born King of all the world.
  And all the angels sang for him,
  The bells of heaven rang for him,
  For a child was born King of all the world.

2 Soon the shepherds came that way
  Where the baby lay
  And were kneeling, kneeling by his side,
  And their hearts believed again
  For the peace of men,
  For a boy was born King of all the world.

  And all the angels sang for him, . . .

Joy Webb

*Words and music ©
Salvationist Publishing
and Supplies Ltd, London.
Used by permission.*

*Salvation Army songster
Joy Webb wrote the words
and music of this carol,
which is about a calm,
still earth, a rejoicing
heaven, shepherds who
learn to believe in peace
again, and a boy born to
be king.*

---

50 *I warm my son upon my breast*
      (Nkosi Jesus)

1 I warm my son upon my breast
  As Mary, Mary warmèd you,
  O, Nkosi Jesus, O, Nkosi Jesus.
  I feel his life, I feel his strength
  And his gentle quiet breathing.
  O, Nkosi Jesus, O, Nkosi Jesus.

Rae Tomlin

*Words © Rae Tomlin.
Used by permission of
Blandford, a Cassell
imprint.*

2 I hear my people singing their song,
  Singing, singing in the wind,
  O, Nkosi Jesus, O, Nkosi Jesus.
  The sighing of the yellow grass
  Keeps him softly, sweetly dreaming.
  O, Nkosi Jesus, O, Nkosi Jesus.

3 The kaffir-boom lifts her arms above,
  Praising, praising only you,
  O, Nkosi Jesus, O, Nkosi Jesus.
  O give us your hope, O give us your strength,
  O give us, give us gentle love.
  O, Nkosi Jesus, O, Nkosi Jesus.

The story of the Nativity is seen through the eyes of an African mother. 'Nkosi' is a Zulu word for king, chief or lord. The 'kaffir-boom' is the African 'lucky-bean tree'.

This beautiful lullaby, with its exquisitely shaped melody by Edith Hugo Bosman, needs to be sung with the utmost simplicity.

---

51 I wonder as I wander, out under the sky

1 I wonder as I wander, out under the sky,
  How Jesus the Saviour did come for to die
  For poor or'n'ry people like you and like I . . .
  I wonder as I wander, out under the sky.

2 When Mary bore Jesus, 'twas in a cow's stall,
  With wise men and animals and shepherds and all.
  But high from the heavens a star's light did fall,
  And the promise of ages it then did recall.

3 If Jesus had wanted for any wee thing,
  A star in the sky or a bird on the wing,
  Or all of God's angels in heaven for to sing,
  He could surely have had it, 'cause he was the king.

4 I wonder as I wander, out under the sky,
  How Jesus the Saviour did come for to die
  For poor or'n'ry people like you and like I . . .
  I wonder as I wander, out under the sky.

North Carolina traditional

An unusual song, written in the first person singular and often performed as a solo. The words are deliberately ungrammatical and 'rustic'; and the unresolved, unconventional tune makes a perfect match.

---

52 Jesus, good above all other

1 Jesus, good above all other,
  Gentle child of gentle mother,
  In a stable born our brother,
  Give us grace to persevere.

2 Jesus, cradled in a manger,
  For us facing every danger,
  Living as a homeless stranger,
  Make we thee our King most dear.

Percy Dearmer (1867–1936)

Percy Dearmer wrote this hymn for children, to go with the 14th-century German carol tune 'Quem Pastores Laudavere', which was

3 Jesus, for thy people dying,
  Risen Master, death defying,
  Lord in heaven, thy grace supplying,
  Keep us to thy presence near.

4 Jesus, who our sorrows bearest,
  All our thoughts and hopes thou sharest,
  Thou to us the truth declarest;
  Help us all thy truth to hear.

5 Lord, in all our doings guide us;
  Pride and hate shall ne'er divide us;
  We'll go on with thee beside us,
  And with joy we'll persevere!

*traditionally sung around
the crib in church during
the Christmas Mystery
plays.*

---

53   *Jesus, Son of God,*
well-spring of forgiveness

Jesus, Son of God, well-spring of forgiveness,
Jesus, Son of God, born in Bethlehem.

Jacques Berthier

*Words and music ©
Ateliers et Presses de
Taizé, 71250 Taizé
Communauté, France.
Used by permission.*

*Another four-part canon
from Taizé at Christmas
(see 'Gloria', no. 26).*

---

54   *Jesus was born in a stable*
(Good Enough for Him)

1 Jesus was born in a stable:
  There was no room in the inn.
  He had a stall for a cradle;
  That was good enough for him.

2 Cattle asleep in the corner,
  Joseph kept watch from within.
  Can you imagine the sorrow?
  That was good enough for him.

3 No kingly robes for his vesture,
  No royal hall for this One.
  But Mary fondled her treasure,
  For he was God's dear Son.

4 Jesus was born in a stable:
  There was no room in the inn.
  He had a stall for a cradle;
  That was good enough for him.

  And that was good enough for him.

Peter Chesters

*Words and music © 1960
Joseph Weinberger
Limited. Used by
permission of the
copyright owners.*

*This blues with a slow
insistent rhythm is about
the simple circumstances
of Christ's birth.*

---

55 *Joseph, dearest Joseph mine*

1 Joseph, dearest Joseph mine,
  Help me rock this child of mine;
  God will honour thee and thine
  In heav'n with him, the holy son of Mary.

  Christ was born on Christmas Day,
  On Christmas Day in Israel;
  Mary mother hears the word of Gabriel.
  Eia, Eia,
  Christ is born, the holy son of Mary.

2 Gladly will I, lady mine,
  Help to rock this child of thine;
  God's own heav'nly light shall shine
  On me and mine, from him, the son of Mary.

  Christ was born on Christmas Day, . . .

3 Peace and pardon bless us all,
  God in heaven is God in stall;
  There he lies, a babe so small,
  To ransom us, the holy son of Mary.

  Christ was born on Christmas Day, . . .

4 Thou art come to keep my heart,
  Love, th'eternal Word thou art,
  Help me now to play my part
  And welcome him, the holy son of Mary.

  Christ was born on Christmas Day, . . .

5 Sweet thou art, O Babe of Grace,
  Poor thou art, and poor thy place,
  Yet in godhead turn thy face
  To smile and save, O holy Son of Mary.

  Christ was born on Christmas Day, . . .

*German, 15th century,
tr. Elizabeth Poston*

*An imaginary
conversation between
Joseph and Mary. Both
tune and words were
written to be sung round
the crib as part of a
German Mystery play.*

---

56 *Joy to the world! the Lord is come*

1 Joy to the world! the Lord is come;
  Let earth receive her King;
  Let ev'ry heart prepare him room,
  And heav'n and nature sing,
  And heav'n and nature sing,
  And heav'n, and heav'n and nature sing.

Isaac Watts (1673–1748)

*Isaac Watts's words and
Handel's tune 'Antioch'
have been enjoying a
popular revival in recent*

2 Joy to the world! the Saviour reigns;
Let us our songs employ;
While fields and floods, rocks, hills and plains,
Repeat the sounding joy,
Repeat the sounding joy,
Repeat, repeat the sounding joy.

3 No more let sin and sorrow grow,
Nor thorns infest the ground;
He comes to make his blessings flow
Far as the curse is found,
Far as the curse is found,
Far as, far as the curse is found.

4 He rules the world with truth and grace,
And makes the nations prove
The glories of his righteousness,
And wonders of his love,
And wonders of his love,
And wonders, and wonders of his love.

*years, largely through
black-led churches, whose
gospel choirs have made a
great impact with them,
particularly on televised
gospel services, and
programmes like Channel
4's* People Get Ready *and
BBC TV's* Rock Gospel
Show.

---

57 *King Jesus hath a garden, full of divers flow'rs*

1 King Jesus hath a garden, full of divers flow'rs,
Where I go culling posies gay, all times and hours.

 There naught is heard but Paradise bird,
 Harp, dulcimer, lute, with cymbal,
 Trump and tymbal, and the tender, soothing flute;
 With cymbal, trump and tymbal,
 And the tender, soothing flute.

2 The Lily, white in blossom there, is Chastity:
The Violet, with sweet perfume, Humility.

 There naught is heard but Paradise bird, . . .

3 The bonny Damask-rose is known as Patience:
The blithe and thrifty Marygold, Obedience.

 There naught is heard but Paradise bird, . . .

4 The Crown Imperial bloometh too in yonder place,
'Tis Charity, of stock divine, the flower of grace.

 There naught is heard but Paradise bird, . . .

5 Yet, 'mid the brave, the bravest prize of all may claim
The Star of Bethlem — Jesus — blessèd be his Name!

 There naught is heard but Paradise bird, . . .

*Dutch, 17th century,
tr. George Ratcliffe
Woodward (1848–1934)*

*A traditional Dutch carol,
harmonized by Charles
Wood, naming the flowers
that grow in Jesus' garden
in Paradise, the spiritual
virtues that are associated
with them, and the
musical instruments the
angels are playing.*

6 Ah! Jesu Lord, my heal and weal, my bliss complete,
   Make thou my heart thy garden-plot, fair, trim and neat.

   That I may hear this musick clear:
   Harp, dulcimer, lute, with cymbal,
   Trump and tymbal, and the tender, soothing flute;
   With cymbal, trump and tymbal,
   And the tender, soothing flute.

---

58 *Les anges dans nos campagnes*

1 Les anges dans nos campagnes
   Ont entonné l'hymne des cieux;
   Et l'écho de nos montagnes
   Redit ce chant mélodieux:

      Gloria in excelsis Deo!
      Gloria in excelsis Deo!

2 Bergers, pour qui cette fête?
   Quel est l'objet de tous ces chants?
   Quel vainqueur, quelle conquête
   Mérite ces cris triomphants?

      Gloria in excelsis Deo! . . .

3 Ils annoncent la naissance
   Du libérateur d'Israël,
   Et pleins de reconnaissance
   Chantent en ce jour solennel.

      Gloria in excelsis Deo! . . .

French, 18th century

The original of 'Angels, from the realms of glory' (no. 5). Another English-language version is 'Shepherds in the field abiding' (no. 90), sung in Canada.

---

59 *Light, scattering the darkness*

1 Light, scattering the darkness,
   Shines on Christmas night;
   Wise men begin their journey,
   Following the light.

      Star, twinkling in the heavens,
      Beckon humankind:
      'Seek the Lord and you will find
      the light of the world.'

*Patrick Appleford
(b. 1925)*

*Words and music
© Patrick Appleford 1990*

The light that led the wise men to Bethlehem all those years ago is still

2 Light, piercing through the darkness
   Deep within us all,
   Shine clearly on our pathway;
   Guide us lest we fall.

   Star, twinkling in the heavens, . . .

3 Christ, light of every nation,
   Teach the world your ways;
   Truth, justice, love and mercy
   Make our songs of praise.

   Star, twinkling in the heavens, . . .

*shining, and calling all of
us to search for Christ
today.*

---

60 *Little donkey, little donkey*

1 Little donkey, little donkey,
   On a dusty road,
   Got to keep on plodding onward
   With your precious load:

2 Been a long time, little donkey,
   Through the winter's night —
   Don't give up now, little donkey,
   Bethlehem's in sight.

   Ring out those bells tonight,
   Bethlehem, Bethlehem;
   Follow that star tonight,
   Bethlehem, Bethlehem!

3 Little donkey, little donkey,
   Had a heavy day —
   Little donkey, carry Mary
   Safely on her way.

   Little donkey, carry Mary
   Safely on her way.

Eric Boswell

*Words and music © 1959
Chappell Music Ltd. Used
by permission of Chappell
Music Ltd and
International Music
Publications.*

*Written in 1959, a song
that used to make it
regularly into the Top
Twenty at Christmas time,
particularly in the days of
BBC Radio's* Children's
Favourites *in the 1950s
and 1960s. It is printed
here in G.C. Westcott's
arrangement.*

---

61 *Little Jesus, sweetly sleep, do not stir (Rocking)*

1 Little Jesus, sweetly sleep, do not stir;
   We will lend a coat of fur.
   We will rock you, rock you, rock you,
   We will rock you, rock you, rock you:
   See the fur to keep you warm,
   Snugly round your tiny form.

*Czech, tr. Percy Dearmer
(1867–1936)*

*This traditional Czech
melody, arranged here by
Martin Shaw (1875 –*

2 Mary's little baby, sleep, sweetly sleep,
Sleep in comfort, slumber deep.
We will rock you, rock you, rock you,
We will rock you, rock you, rock you:
We will serve you all we can,
Darling, darling little man.

*1958), is very similar to
nursery rhyme tunes for
'Twinkle, twinkle, little
star' and 'Baa baa black
sheep', and is easily
taught to very young
children; but whoever
sings it should do so
slowly, softly and
smoothly.*

62 *Lo! he comes with clouds descending*

1 Lo! he comes with clouds descending,
Once for favoured sinners slain;
Thousand thousand saints attending
Swell the triumph of his train:
Alleluya!
Alleluya!
Alleluya!
God appears, on earth to reign.

2 Every eye shall now behold him
Robed in dreadful majesty;
Those who set at nought and sold him,
Pierced and nailed him to the tree,
Deeply wailing,
Deeply wailing,
Deeply wailing
Shall the true Messiah see.

3 Those dear tokens of his passion
Still his dazzling body bears,
Cause of endless exultation
To his ransomed worshippers:
With what rapture,
With what rapture,
With what rapture
Gaze we on those glorious scars!

4 Yea, amen! let all adore thee,
High on thine eternal throne;
Saviour, take the power and glory:
Claim the kingdom for thine own:
O come quickly!
O come quickly!
O come quickly!
Alleluya! Come, Lord, come!

*J. Cennick (1718–55) and
Charles Wesley (1707–88)*

*With his 1758
amendments, Charles
Wesley toned down
considerably the rather
crudely passionate hymn,
based on Revelation 1.7,
which Cennick had written
in 1750. Subsequent
editors made even further
revisions, but the words
remain full of apocalyptic,
ominous images, and have
great grandeur which,
combined with the
tremendous tune,
'Helmsley', make this a
splendid processional
hymn.*

63 Long time ago in Bethlehem (Mary's Boy Child)

1 Long time ago in Bethlehem,
   So the Holy Bible say,
   Mary's boy-child, Jesus Christ,
   Was born on Christmas Day.

   Hark now, hear the angels sing —
   A new king born today!
   And we may live for evermore
   Because of Christmas Day.
   Trumpets sound and angels sing —
   Listen to what they say,
   That we may live for evermore
   Because of Christmas Day.

2 While shepherds watch their flocks by night,
   Them see a bright new shining star;
   Them hear a choir sing —
   The music seems to come from afar.

3 Now Joseph and his wife Mary
   Come to Bethlehem that night;
   She have no place to bear her child —
   Not a single room was in sight.

   Hark now, hear the angels sing . . .

4 By and by they find a little nook
   In a stable all forlorn,
   And in a manger cold and dark,
   Mary's little boy was born.

5 Long time ago in Bethlehem,
   So the Holy Bible say,
   Mary's boy-child, Jesus Christ,
   Was born on Christmas Day.

   Hark now, hear the angels sing . . .

   Yes, we may live for evermore
   Because of Christmas Day.

Jester Hairston

*Words and music ©
Bourne Music Ltd. Used
by permission.*

*A popular West Indian
carol that has also
appeared in the Top
Twenty. It may need
some practice, because the
way the words fit the notes
varies from verse to verse.
One possibility would be
to have the verses sung by
a soloist; but in any case,
this music benefits from a
flexible approach to the
rhythm.
   The final two lines are
sung to the last four-and-
a-quarter bars of the
refrain.*

64 Love came down at Christmas

1 Love came down at Christmas,
   Love all lovely, love divine;
   Love was born at Christmas,
   Star and angels gave the sign.

*Christina Rossetti
(1830–94)*

2 Worship we the Godhead,
  Love incarnate, love divine;
  Worship we our Jesus:
  But wherewith for sacred sign?

3 Love shall be our token,
  Love be yours and love be mine;
  Love to God and neighbour,
  Love for plea and gift and sign.

*Written in 1885, this is a
beautiful, short hymn,
best sung in unison, that
says a lot in very few
words.*

  *'Garton' is a traditional
Irish air, arranged here
by David Iliff.*

---

65 *Lully, lulla, thou little tiny child (Coventry Carol)*

Lully, lulla, thou little tiny child,
By by, lully lullay.

1 O sisters too,
  How may we do
  For to preserve this day?
  This poor youngling,
  For whom we sing,
  By by, lully lullay!

2 Herod, the king,
  In his raging,
  Chargèd he hath this day
  His men of might,
  In his own sight,
  All young children to slay.

3 That woe is me,
  Poor child for thee!
  And ever morn and may,
  For thy parting
  Neither say nor sing
  By by, lully lullay!

Lully, lulla, thou little tiny child,
By by, lully, lullay.

*Pageant of the Shearmen
and Tailors, Coventry,
15th century*

*Part of the mediaeval
Coventry Plays, the words
and music are laden with
impending doom, for all
the innocent children
born at this time who will
be massacred by King
Herod.*

  *The music has been
arranged by Martin Shaw
(1875–1958).*

---

66 *Magnificat anima mea dominum*

All Magnificat anima mea dominum. *(hum)*
A   My soul proclaims the gréatness of thé Lórd
All Magnificat! *(hum)*
B   And my spirit exults in Gód my sáviour;
All Magnificat!

Jacques Berthier

All	Magnificat anima mea dominum. *(hum)*
A	Because he has looked upon his lówly hándmáid.
All	Magnificat! *(hum)*
B	Yes, from this day forward all generations will call me blessèd,
	for the Almighty has done gréat things for mé.
All	Magnificat!

The Magnificat, or Song of Mary at the Visitation, is traditionally associated with our preparation for the coming of Christ. This version comes from the Taizé Community.

All	Magnificat anima mea dominum. *(hum)*
A	Holy ís hís náme,
All	Magnificat! *(hum)*
B	And his mercy reaches from age to age for thóse who féar him.
All	Magnificat!

All	Magnificat anima mea dominum. *(hum)*
A	He has shown the pówer of hís árm,
All	Magnificat! *(hum)*
B	He has routed the proúd of héart.
All	Magnificat!

All	Magnificat anima mea dominum. *(hum)*
A	He has pulled down prínces from théir thrónes
All	Magnificat! *(hum)*
B	And exálted the lówly.
All	Magnificat!

All	Magnificat anima mea dominum. *(hum)*
A	The hungry he has fílled with góod thíngs,
All	Magnificat! *(hum)*
B	The rich sent émpty awáy.
All	Magnificat!

All	Magnificat anima mea dominum. *(hum)*
A	He has come to the help of Ísrael hís sérvant,
All	Magnificat! *(hum)*
B	Mindful of his mercy to Abraham and to his descéndants for éver.
All	Magnificat!

---

67 *Make straight in the desert a highway for our God*

1 Make straight in the desert a highway for our God;
John echoes Isaiah: prepare the way of the Lord.
Look, look for his coming to set his people free;
Christ is the Messiah whose glory all shall see.

2 Crowds flocked to the desert and found young John inspired;
His passionate preaching made clear what God required:
Turn, turn to the Father, and listen to his Word;
Make straight in the desert a highway for our God.

Patrick Appleford
(b. 1925)

Words and music ©
Patrick Appleford 1990

Using biblical phrases from Isaiah 40 and 61, and the story and message of John the Baptist in the gospels,

44

3 Christ went to the desert and humbly was baptized.
John witnessed the glory before his very eyes:
Joy, joy with the Father, the Spirit and the Son,
Signs there in the desert God's highway was begun.

Patrick Appleford's Advent hymn says: make your heart a highway for God to come to you.

4 John would not be silenced by violence or fear.
John, murdered in prison, still speaks to those who
    hear:
Learn, learn from the Baptist; hold fast to what is
    true;
Make your heart a highway for God to come to you.

5 Yours, Lord, is the glory, let all your saints rejoice.
John was the forerunner with true prophetic voice.
Great, great is your glory, yet you come down to
    earth,
Heav'n rings with the echoes of joy at Jesu's birth.

---

68 *Make way, make way*

1 Make way, make way,
For Christ the king in splendour arrives;
Fling wide the gates
And welcome him into your lives.

  Make way, (make way,)
  For the King of Kings;
  Make way, (make way,)
  And let his kingdom in!

Graham Kendrick

Words and music © Graham Kendrick/ Thankyou Music. Used by permission.

Based on Isaiah 40.3−5 and Luke 4.18−19 (see also 'Hark the glad sound!', no. 33). Graham Kendrick's lively, evangelical hymns have won renown and popularity through being broadcast regularly on television and radio.

2 He comes the broken hearts to heal,
The prisoners to free;
The deaf shall hear, the lame shall dance,
The blind shall see.

  Make way, (make way,) . . .

3 And those who mourn with heavy hearts,
Who weep and sigh,
With laughter, joy and royal crown
He'll beautify.

  Make way, (make way,) . . .

4 We call you now to worship him
As Lord of all,
To have no gods before him —
Their thrones must fall!

  Make way, (make way,) . . .

---

69 Mary had a baby

1 Mary had a baby,
   Yes, Lord.
   Mary had a baby,
   Yes, my Lord.
   Mary had a baby,
   Yes, Lord.
   The people keep a-coming
   And the train done gone.

2 What did she name him?
   Yes, Lord . . .

3 Mary named him Jesus,
   Yes, Lord . . .

4 Where was he born?
   Yes, Lord . . .

5 Born in a stable,
   Yes, Lord . . .

6 Where did Mary lay him?
   Yes, Lord . . .

7 Laid him in a manger,
   Yes, Lord . . .

St Helena Island spiritual

*Words and music ©
David Iliff. Used by
permission of A. & C.
Black.*

*A version of a traditional
spiritual, and another one
that children can add to,
building up the Christmas
story (see 'Here we go up
to Bethlehem', no. 35).*
   *The tune lends itself to
accompaniment on
percussion instruments.*

---

70 Masters in this hall

1 Masters in this hall,
   Hear ye news today
   Brought from over sea,
   And ever I you pray:

   Nowell! Nowell! Nowell!
   Nowell sing we clear!
   Holpen are all folk on earth,
   Born is God's Son so dear:
   Nowell! Nowell! Nowell!
   Nowell sing we loud!
   God today hath poor folk raised
   And cast adown the proud.

2 Going o'er the hills,
   Through the milk-white snow,
   Heard I ewès bleat
   While the wind did blow:

   Nowell! Nowell! Nowell! . . .

William Morris (1834–96)

*Morris wrote these words
about 1860, for an old
French tune obtained at
Chartres by Edmund
Sedding, an architect with
whom Morris was working.
Sedding published the
piece in his* Antient
Christmas Carols.
   *Such a long carol can
be useful for a procession;
the different characters
can be taken by different
voices or groups, with
everyone joining in the
chorus.*

46

3 Shepherds many an one
  Sat among the sheep,
  No man spake more word
  Than they had been asleep:

      Nowell! Nowell! Nowell! . . .

4 Quoth I, 'Fellows mine,
  Why this guise sit ye?
  Making but dull cheer,
  Shepherds though ye be?

      Nowell! Nowell! Nowell! . . .

5 'Shepherds should of right
  Leap and dance and sing,
  Thus to see ye sit,
  It is a right strange thing':

      Nowell! Nowell! Nowell! . . .

6 Quoth these fellows then,
  'To Bethlem town we go,
  To see a mighty lord
  Lie in a manger low':

      Nowell! Nowell! Nowell! . . .

7 Then to Bethlem town
  We went two and two,
  And in a sorry place
  Heard the oxen low:

      Nowell! Nowell! Nowell! . . .

8 Therein did we see
  A sweet and goodly may
  And a fair old man,
  Upon the straw she lay:

      Nowell! Nowell! Nowell! . . .

9 And a little child
  On her arm had she,
  'Wot ye who this is?'
  Said the hinds to me:

      Nowell! Nowell! Nowell! . . .

10 This is Christ the Lord,
   Masters be ye glad!
   Christmas is come in,
   And no folk should be sad:

      Nowell! Nowell! Nowell! . . .

71 *No crowded eastern street*

1 No crowded eastern street,
  No sound of passing feet;
  Far to the left and far to right
  The prairie snows spread fair and white;
  Yet still to us is born tonight
  The child, the King of Glory.

2 No rock-hewn place of peace
  Shared with the gentle beasts,
  But sturdy farmhouse, stout and warm,
  With stable, shed and great red barn;
  And still to us is born tonight
  The child, the King of Glory.

3 No blaze of heavenly fire,
  No bright celestial choir:
  Only the starlight as of old,
  Crossed by the planes' flash, red and gold;
  Yet still to us is born tonight
  The child, the King of Glory.

4 No kings with gold and grain,
  No stately camel train;
  Yet in his presence all may stand
  With loving heart and willing hand;
  For still to us is born tonight
  The child, the King of Glory.

Frieda Major (b. 1891)

*A Canadian carol, simple
and effective, which
places the Christmas story
firmly in the 20th century.
'Heritage' is by Robert J.
B. Fleming (b. 1921).*

---

72 *Now the holly bears a berry as white as the milk (Sans Day Carol)*

1 Now the holly bears a berry as white as the milk,
  And Mary bore Jesus, who was wrapped up in silk:

  And Mary bore Jesus Christ
  Our Saviour for to be,
  And the first tree in the greenwood,
  It was the holly, holly! holly!
  And the first tree in the greenwood,
  It was the holly.

2 Now the holly bears a berry as green as the grass,
  And Mary bore Jesus, who died on the cross:

  And Mary bore Jesus Christ . . .

*Cornish traditional,
collated Percy Dearmer
(1867–1936)*

*Called the Sans Day Carol
after the place where it
was found, St Day, in
Cornwall, named after a
Breton saint whose cult
had spread there. The
Cornish words and tune
were known at St Day for
years before they were*

3 Now the holly bears a berry as black as the coal,
  And Mary bore Jesus, who died for us all:

  And Mary bore Jesus Christ . . .

4 Now the holly bears a berry, as blood is it red,
  Then trust we our Saviour, who rose from the dead:

  And Mary bore Jesus Christ . . .

---

73 *O come, all ye faithful*

1 O come, all ye faithful,
  Joyful and triumphant,
  O come ye, O come ye to Bethlehem;
  Come and behold him
  Born the King of Angels:

      O come, let us adore him,
      O come, let us adore him,
      O come, let us adore him, Christ the Lord!

2 God of God,
  Light of Light,
  Lo! he abhors not the Virgin's womb;
  Very God,
  Begotten, not created:

      O come, let us adore him, . . .

3 See how the shepherds,
  Summoned to his cradle,
  Leaving their flocks, draw nigh with lowly fear;
  We too will thither
  Bend our joyful footsteps:

      O come, let us adore him, . . .

4 Lo! star-led chieftains,
  Magi, Christ adoring,
  Offer him incense, gold, and myrrh;
  We to the Christ Child
  Bring our heart's oblations:

      O come, let us adore him, . . .

5 Child, for us sinners
  Poor and in the manger,
  Fain we embrace thee, with awe and love;
  Who would not love thee,
  Loving us so dearly?

      O come, let us adore him, . . .

*discovered, collected,
translated and published.*

*John Francis Wade
(1711–86),
tr. Frederick Oakley
(1802–80) and others*

*Neither the irregular
metre of the lines nor the
lack of rhyme has
prevented this carol from
becoming one of the most
popular of all, especially
with its affirmative final
verse, traditionally only
sung on Christmas day
itself (though on another
day, it is always possible
to sing 'Born that happy
morning').*

*'Adeste Fideles' is by an
unknown composer, but
very possibly it was also by
John Wade, who wrote the
original Latin words.*

6 Sing, choirs of angels,
  Sing in exultation,
  Sing, all ye citizens of heaven above;
  Glory to God
  In the Highest:

  O come, let us adore him, . . .

7 Yea, Lord, we greet thee,
  Born this happy morning,
  Jesu, to thee be glory given;
  Word of the Father,
  Now in flesh appearing:

  O come, let us adore him, . . .

---

74   *O come, O come, Emmanuel*

1 O come, O come, Emmanuel,
  And ransom captive Israel,
  That mourns in lonely exile here,
  Until the Son of God appear.

  Rejoice! Rejoice! Emmanuel
  Shall come to thee, O Israel.

2 O come, thou Rod of Jesse, free
  Thine own from Satan's tyranny;
  From depths of hell thy people save,
  And give them victory o'er the grave.

  Rejoice! Rejoice! Emmanuel . . .

3 O come, thou Dayspring, come and cheer
  Our spirits by thine advent here;
  Disperse the gloomy clouds of night,
  And death's dark shadows put to flight.

  Rejoice! Rejoice! Emmanuel . . .

4 O come, thou Key of David, come,
  And open wide our heavenly home;
  Make safe the way that leads on high,
  And close the path to misery.

  Rejoice! Rejoice! Emmanuel . . .

5 O come, O come, thou Lord of Might,
  Who to thy tribes, on Sinai's height,
  In ancient times didst give the law
  In cloud and majesty and awe.

  Rejoice! Rejoice! Emmanuel . . .

Latin, c. 13th century,
tr. John Mason Neale
(1818–66)

Words based on the
ancient Advent antiphons
of the mediaeval Church,
with each verse
addressing Christ by a
different Old Testament
title.
   'Veni Immanuel',
arranged here by Noël
Tredinnick, strongly
suggests plainsong, and is
more effective sung
lightly, following the
natural rhythm of the
spoken word, rather than
in stiff regular measures.

75 *Of the Father's heart begotten*

1 Of the Father's heart begotten,
Ere the world from chaos rose,
He is Alpha: from that fountain
All that is and hath been flows;
He is Omega, of all things
Yet to come the mystic close,
Evermore and evermore.

2 By his word was all created;
He commanded and 'twas done;
Earth and sky and boundless ocean,
Universe of three in one,
All that sees the moon's soft radiance,
All that breathes beneath the sun,
Evermore and evermore.

3 He assumed this mortal body,
Frail and feeble, doomed to die,
That the race from dust created
Might not perish utterly,
Which the dreadful law had sentenced
In the depths of hell to lie,
Evermore and evermore.

4 This is he, whom seer and sibyl
Sang in ages long gone by;
This is he of old revealèd
In the page of prophecy;
Lo! he comes, the promised saviour;
Let the world his praises cry!
Evermore and evermore.

5 Let the storm and summer sunshine,
Gliding stream and sounding shore,
Sea and forest, frost and zephyr,
Day and night their Lord adore;
Let creation join to laud thee
Through the ages evermore,
Evermore and evermore.

6 Sing, ye heights of heaven, his praises;
Angels and archangels, sing!
Wheresoe'er ye be, ye faithful,
Let your joyous anthems ring,
Every tongue his name confessing,
Countless voices answering,
Evermore and evermore . . .

*Prudentius (348–413),
tr. R. F. Davis
(1866–1937)*

*The oldest of all Christmas
hymns, often used as a
processional. It is not just
about Christ's
Incarnation, but is a
triumphant assertion of
his glory and oneness
with God, and all
creation is invited to join
in praise.*

*'Divinum Mysterium' is
a mediaeval melody
found in* Piae Cantiones
*(1582). It is best sung in
unison, and moderately
fast.*

76 *O leave your sheep*

1 O leave your sheep,
   Where ewes with lambs are feeding;
   You shepherds, hear
   Our message of good cheer.
   No longer weep;
   The angel tidings heeding,
   To Bethlem haste away.
   Our Lord, (our Lord,)
   Our Lord, (our Lord,)
   Our Lord is born this happy day.
   Our Lord, (our Lord,)
   Our Lord, (our Lord,)
   Our Lord is born this happy day.

2 For love lies there
   Within a lowly manger —
   The infant poor
   Whom angel hosts adore!
   Such perfect care
   Has saved us all from danger
   And brought us to the fold.
   Now see, (now see,)
   Now see, (now see,)
   God's faithful love revealed of old.
   Now see, (now see,)
   Now see, (now see,)
   God's faithful love revealed of old.

3 You wise men three,
   Arrayed in royal splendour,
   True homage pay:
   Your king is born today!
   The star you see
   Its radiance must surrender
   Before our sun most bright.
   Your gifts, (your gifts,)
   Your gifts, (your gifts,)
   Your gifts are precious in his sight.
   Your gifts, (your gifts,)
   Your gifts, (your gifts,)
   Your gifts are precious in his sight.

John Rutter, from the French

An English version of the traditional French carol 'Quittez, pasteurs'. In the last six lines of each verse, the words in brackets may be sung by a second part.

'Angevin' first appeared in print in the 19th century. It needs to be sung smoothly, with the long notes given their full value, but to keep moving.

4 O Spirit blessed,
  The source of life eternal,
  Our souls inspire
  With your celestial fire!
  We make our guest
  The Christ, the Lord supernal,
  And sing the peace on earth
  God gives, (God gives,)
  God gives, (God gives,)
  God gives us by this holy birth.
  God gives, (God gives,)
  God gives, (God gives,)
  God gives us by this holy birth.

---

77 *O little one sweet, O little one mild*

1 O little one sweet, O little one mild
  Your father's purpose you have fulfilled;
  That we might understand his care
  Our fragile human life you share,
  O little one sweet, O little one mild.

2 O little one sweet, O little one mild
  With joy you have the whole world filled;
  You came to us from heaven's domain,
  To bring us comfort in our pain,
  O little one sweet, O little one mild.

3 O little one sweet, O little one mild,
  In you love's beauties are distilled;
  Then light in us your love's bright flame
  That we may give you back the same,
  O little one sweet, O little one mild.

*Samuel Scheidt
(1587–1654),
tr. Patrick Appleford*

*A German carol which
first appeared in 1650; a
hymn of praise and
prayer to the baby in the
manger. Here it is in a
new translation.*

*Harmonized as a
chorale by Johann
Sebastian Bach, it should
be sung slowly and gently.*

---

78 *O little town of Bethlehem*

1 O little town of Bethlehem,
  How still we see thee lie!
  Above thy deep and dreamless sleep
  The silent stars go by.
  Yet in thy dark streets shineth
  The everlasting light;
  The hopes and fears of all the years
  Are met in thee to-night.

Phillips Brooks (1835–93)

*Phillips Brooks, a great
American preacher, wrote
this carol for his Sunday
School children. The
words stir up, even in the
most cynical of us, deep*

2 O morning stars, together
   Proclaim the holy birth,
   And praises sing to God the King,
   And peace to all on earth;
   For Christ is born of Mary;
   And, gathered all above,
   While mortals sleep, the angels keep
   Their watch of wondering love.

3 How silently, how silently,
   The wondrous gift is given!
   So God imparts to human hearts
   The blessings of his heaven.
   No ear may hear his coming;
   But in this world of sin,
   Where meek souls will receive him, still
   The dear Christ enters in.

4 Where children pure and happy
   Pray to the blessèd Child,
   Where misery cries out to thee,
   Son of the mother mild;
   Where charity stands watching
   And faith holds wide the door,
   The dark night wakes, the glory breaks,
   And Christmas comes once more.

5 O holy child of Bethlehem,
   Descend to us, we pray;
   Cast out our sin, and enter in,
   Be born in us today.
   We hear the Christmas angels
   The great glad tidings tell:
   O come to us, abide with us,
   Our Lord Emmanuel.

*feelings of hope that the
Christmas story should be
true.*

*'Forest Green' is the
name given by Ralph
Vaughan Williams to the
traditional English tune
'The Ploughboy's Dream',
which matches the words
perfectly. In each verse,
the first note of the
penultimate line is longer
than many people think!*

---

79 *O Mary most holy
(Lourdes Hymn)*

1 O Mary most holy, you brought forth God's Son;
   Your joy is the joy of all ages to come.

   Ave, ave, ave Maria,
   Ave, ave, ave Maria.

2 To you, by an angel, the Father made known
   The grace of his Spirit, the gift of his Son.

   Ave, ave, ave Maria, . . .

3 Your child is the Saviour, all hope lies in him:
   He gives us new life and redeems us from sin.

   Ave, ave, ave Maria, . . .

*The Venerable Bede,
tr. and paraphrased*

*A Nativity hymn from
Lourdes, France. Pilgrims
in their thousands visit
the grotto where, in 1858,
Bernadette Soubirous had
visions of the Blessed
Virgin Mary, and a spring
of healing water
appeared. Sung in
procession by children
dressed in white, the*

4 In glory for ever now close to your Son,
  All ages will praise you for all God has done.

    Ave, ave, ave Maria, . . .

*hymn is also associated
with first communions.
   The tune is a
traditional French
melody, heard on
carillons everywhere
around Lourdes.*

80   *Once in royal David's city*

1 Once in royal David's city
  Stood a lowly cattle shed,
  Where a mother laid her baby
  In a manger for his bed:
  Mary was that mother mild,
  Jesus Christ her little child.

2 He came down to earth from heaven
  Who is God and Lord of all,
  And his shelter was a stable,
  And his cradle was a stall:
  With the poor and mean and lowly,
  Lived on earth our Saviour holy.

3 And through all his wondrous childhood
  Day by day like us he grew;
  He was little, weak and helpless,
  Tears and smiles like us he knew:
  And he feeleth for our sadness,
  And he shareth in our gladness.

4 And our eyes at last shall see him
  Through his own redeeming love,
  For that child so dear and gentle
  Is our Lord in heaven above:
  And he leads his children on
  To the place where he is gone.

5 Not in that poor lowly stable,
  With the oxen standing by,
  We shall see him: but in heaven,
  Set at God's right hand on high,
  Where like stars his children crowned,
  All in white shall wait around.

*C. F. Alexander
(1818–95)*

*Not written by Mrs
Alexander as a Christmas
carol, but to illustrate part
of the Apostles' Creed in
her* Hymns for Little
Children *(1848). A skilful
mingling of Bible story
and Christian theology, it
has become a traditional
part of Christmas, partly
through being chosen by
Eric Milner-White to begin
his especially devised
Festival of Nine Lessons
and Carols from King's
College. This gift to the
townspeople of Cambridge
is now a gift to a far
wider audience,
broadcast live on BBC
Radio every Christmas for
over fifty years.
  The tune 'Irby', by H. G.
Gauntlett, has been
harmonized by A. H.
Mann (1850–1929).*

81 On Christmas night, all Christians sing (Sussex Carol)

1 On Christmas night, all Christians sing
   To hear the news the angels bring:
   On Christmas night, all Christians sing
   To hear the news the angels bring:
   News of great joy, news of great mirth,
   News of our merciful King's birth.

2 Then why should we on earth be so sad,
   Since our Redeemer made us glad?
   Then why should we on earth be so sad,
   Since our Redeemer made us glad?
   When from our sin he set us free,
   All for to gain our liberty.

3 When sin departs before his grace,
   Then life and health come in its place;
   When sin departs before his grace
   Then life and health come in its place;
   Angels and we with joy may sing,
   All for to see the new-born King.

4 All out of darkness we have light,
   Which made the angels sing this night;
   All out of darkness we have light,
   Which made the angels sing this night;
   'Glory to God and peace to men,
   Now and for evermore. Amen.'

Sussex traditional,
collected by Ralph
Vaughan Williams
(1872–1958)

A folk carol, collected by
Vaughan Williams at
Monks Gate in Sussex,
whose direct simplicity
emphasizes the happiness
we should all feel at the
birth of the bringer of
mercy and redemption.

82 On Jordan's bank the Baptist's cry

1 On Jordan's bank the Baptist's cry
   Announces that the Lord is nigh;
   Come then and hearken, for he brings
   Glad tidings from the King of Kings.

2 Then cleansed be every Christian breast,
   And furnished for so great a guest!
   Yea, let us each our hearts prepare
   For Christ to come and enter there.

3 For thou art our salvation, Lord,
   Our refuge and our great reward;
   Without thy grace our souls must fade,
   And wither like a flower decayed.

4 To heal the sick stretch out thine hand,
   And bid the fallen sinner stand;
   Shine forth, and let thy light restore
   Earth's own true loveliness once more.

Charles Coffin
(1676–1749), tr. John
Chandler (1806–76)

Written in Latin for
Charles Coffin's Paris
Breviary, this hymn takes
John the Baptist's call to
the people of Israel to
repent and prepare for
Christ's coming, and
addresses it to us, as we
prepare for Christmas.
'Winchester New' is
adapted from a chorale in
the Musikalisches
Handbuch (Hamburg
1690).

5 All praise, eternal Son, to thee
    Whose advent sets thy people free,
    Whom, with the Father, we adore,
    And Spirit blest, for evermore.

---

83   *O Tannenbaum! O Tannenbaum!*

1 O Tannenbaum! O Tannenbaum!
    Wie grün sind deine Blätter!
    O Tannenbaum! O Tannenbaum!
    Wie grün sind deine Blätter!
    Du grünst nicht nur zur Sommerzeit:
    Nein, auch im Winter, wenn es schneit.
    O Tannenbaum! O Tannenbaum!
    Wie grün sind deine Blätter.

2 O Tannenbaum! O Tannenbaum!
    Du kannst mir sehr gefallen!
    O Tannenbaum! O Tannenbaum!
    Du kannst mir sehr gefallen!
    Wie oft hat nicht zur Weihnachtszeit
    Ein Baum von dir mich hoch erfreit:
    O Tannenbaum! O Tannenbaum!
    Du kannst mir sehr gefallen!

3 O Tannenbaum! O Tannenbaum!
    Dein Kleid will mich was lehren!
    O Tannenbaum! O Tannenbaum!
    Dein Kleid will mich was lehren!
    Die Hoffnung und Beständigkeit
    Gibt Trost und Kraft zu jeder Zeit.
    O Tannenbaum! O Tannenbaum!
    Dein Kleid will mich was lehren!

German traditional

For anyone with German roots, Christmas is not Christmas without this carol, which first appeared in the 19th century.

The tune has become associated with the words of 'The Red Flag' but it is with this traditional German carol that it originally belongs.

---

84   *O worship the Lord in the beauty of holiness!*

1 O worship the Lord in the beauty of holiness!
    Bow down before him, his glory proclaim;
    With gold of obedience, and incense of lowliness,
    Kneel and adore him, the Lord is his name!

2 Low at his feet lay thy burden of carefulness,
    High on his heart he will bear it for thee,
    Comfort thy sorrows, and answer thy prayerfulness,
    Guiding thy steps as may best for thee be.

3 Fear not to enter his courts in the slenderness
    Of the poor wealth thou wouldst reckon as thine:
    Truth in its beauty, and love in its tenderness,
    These are the offerings to lay on his shrine.

J. S. B. Monsell (1811–75)

Many of the poetic allusions are biblical (see Psalm 96.9; Philippians 4.6 and Psalm 30.5). The gifts are given a different interpretation from that of the early Church (see no. 11, 'Bethlehem, of noble cities'), but like Heber's, in 'Brightest and best of the sons of the morning' (no.

4 These, though we bring them in trembling and
    fearfulness,
  He will accept for the name that is dear;
  Mornings of joy give for evenings of tearfulness,
  Trust for our trembling and hope for our fear.

5 O worship the Lord in the beauty of holiness!
  Bow down before him, his glory proclaim;
  With gold of obedience, and incense of lowliness,
  Kneel and adore him, the Lord is his name.

*12), Monsell's purpose is
to teach us to worship God
in the right way.*

*'Was Lebet' is an 18th-
century chorale.*

---

85 *Past three a clock*

    Past three a clock,
    And a cold frosty morning:
    Past three a clock;
    Good morrow, masters all!

1 Born is a baby,
  Gentle as may be,
  Son of th'eternal
  Father supernal.

    Past three a clock, . . .

2 Seraph quire singeth,
  Angel bell ringeth:
  Hark how they rime it,
  Time it, and chime it.

    Past three a clock, . . .

3 Mid earth rejoices
  Hearing such voices
  Ne'ertofore so well
  Carolling Nowell.

    Past three a clock, . . .

4 Hinds o'er the pearly
  Dewy lawn early
  Seek the high stranger
  Laid in the manger.

    Past three a clock, . . .

5 Cheese from the dairy
  Bring they for Mary,
  And, not for money,
  Butter and honey.

    Past three a clock, . . .

*George Ratcliffe
Woodward (1848–1934)
(refrain traditional)*

*Deep mystery and
familiar, homely things
are described side by side
in this quaint Victorian
restoration of a more
ancient carol.*

*The tune is the
traditional English carol
melody 'London Waits'.*

6 Light out of star-land
   Leadeth from far land
   Princes, to meet him,
   Worship and greet him.

   Past three a clock, . . .

7 Myrrh from full coffer,
   Incense they offer:
   Nor is the golden
   Nugget withholden.

   Past three a clock, . . .

8 Thus they: I pray you,
   Up, sirs, nor stay you
   Till ye confess him
   Likewise, and bless him.

   Past three a clock, . . .

---

86 *People, look East. The time is near*

1 People, look East. The time is near
   Of the crowning of the year.
   Make your house fair as you are able,
   Trim the hearth, and set the table.
   People, look East, and sing today:
   Love the Guest is on the way.

2 Furrows, be glad. Though earth is bare,
   One more seed is planted there:
   Give up your strength the seed to nourish,
   That in course the flower may flourish.
   People, look East, and sing today:
   Love the Rose is on the way.

3 Birds, though ye long have ceased to build,
   Guard the nest that must be filled.
   Even the hour when wings are frozen
   He for fledging-time has chosen.
   People, look East, and sing today:
   Love the Bird is on the way.

4 Stars, keep the watch. When night is dim
   One more light the bowl shall brim,
   Shining beyond the frosty weather,
   Bright as sun and moon together.
   People, look East, and sing today:
   Love the Star is on the way.

Eleanor Farjeon
(1881–1965)

*The poet Eleanor Farjeon
rewrote and improved on
an earlier version of the
old Besançon carol
'Chantons, bargies, Noué,
Noué' which began:
'Shepherds, shake off your
drowsy sleep,
Rise, and leave your silly
sheep!'*

5 Angels, announce to man and beast
Him who cometh from the East.
Set every peak and valley humming
With the word, the Lord is coming.
People, look East, and sing today:
Love the Lord is on the way.

87 Rejoice and be merry in songs and in mirth (Gallery Carol)

1 Rejoice and be merry in songs and in mirth,
O praise our Redeemer, all mortals on earth:
For this is the birthday of Jesus our King,
Who brought us salvation — his praises we'll sing!

2 A heavenly vision appeared in the sky,
Vast numbers of angels the shepherds did spy,
Proclaiming the birthday of Jesus our King,
Who brought us salvation — his praises we'll sing!

3 Likewise a bright star in the sky did appear,
Which led the Wise Men from the East to draw near;
They found the Messiah, sweet Jesus our King,
Who brought us salvation — his praises we'll sing!

4 And when they were come, they their treasures unfold,
And unto him offered myrrh, incense, and gold.
So blessèd for ever be Jesus our King,
Who brought us salvation — his praises we'll sing!

Old church gallery-book

The words and tune were found in an old handwritten church gallery-book in Dorset by the Rev. L. J. T. Darwall. Much of the west gallery music disappeared when, during the 19th century, organs replaced gallery bands (about which Thomas Hardy wrote, nostalgically, in Under the Greenwood Tree).

88 See amid the winter's snow

1 See amid the winter's snow,
Born for us on earth below;
See the tender Lamb appears,
Promised from eternal years:

    Hail, thou ever-blessèd morn;
    Hail, redemption's happy dawn;
    Sing through all Jerusalem,
    Christ is born in Bethlehem.

2 Lo, within a manger lies
He who built the starry skies;
He who, throned in height sublime,
Sits amid the cherubim:

    Hail, thou ever-blessèd morn; . . .

*Edward Caswall
(1814 – 78)*

*The first two verses are an expression of wonder at the way God's eternal promises are kept by a humble baby in a manger. The next two are a conversation with the rejoicing shepherds, and the last two address the holy child and ask him to teach us to be like him.
'Humility', by John Goss*

60

3 Say, ye holy shepherds, say
  What your joyful news to-day;
  Wherefore have ye left your sheep
  On the lonely mountain steep?

     Hail, thou ever-blessèd morn; . . .

*(1800–80), appeared
with these words in 1871.*

4 'As we watched at dead of night,
  Lo, we saw a wondrous light;
  Angels singing "Peace on earth"
  Told us of the Saviour's birth':

     Hail, thou ever-blessèd morn; . . .

5 Sacred infant, all divine,
  What a tender love was thine,
  Thus to come from highest bliss
  Down to such a world as this:

     Hail, thou ever-blessèd morn; . . .

6 Teach, O teach us, holy child,
  By thy face so meek and mild,
  Teach us to resemble thee,
  In thy sweet humility:

     Hail, thou ever-blessèd morn; . . .

---

89 See him lying on a bed of straw (Calypso Carol)

1 See him lying on a bed of straw:
  A draughty stable with an open door,
  Mary cradling the babe she bore —
  The Prince of Glory is his name:

     O now carry me to Bethlehem
     To see the Lord of love again:
     Just as poor as was the stable then,
     The Prince of Glory when he came.

Michael A. Perry

2 Star of silver, sweep across the skies,
  Show where Jesus in the manger lies.
  Shepherds, swiftly from your stupor rise
  To see the Saviour of the world:

     O now carry me to Bethlehem . . .

3 Angels, sing again the song you sang,
  Sing the glory of God's gracious plan;
  Sing that Bethl'em's little baby can
  Be the saviour of us all:

     O now carry me to Bethlehem . . .

4 Mine are riches, from your poverty,
  From your innocence, eternity;
  Mine forgiveness by your death for me,
  Child of sorrow for my joy:

    O now carry me to Bethlehem . . .

---

90   *Shepherds in the field abiding*

1 Shepherds in the field abiding,
  Tell us, when the seraph bright
  Greeted you with wondrous tiding,
  What you saw and heard that night.

    Gloria in excelsis Deo!
    Gloria in excelsis Deo!

2 We beheld— it is no fable —
  God incarnate, King of Bliss,
  Swathed and cradled in a stable,
  And the angel strain was this:

    Gloria in excelsis Deo! . . .

3 Choristers on high were singing
  Jesus and his virgin birth,
  Heavenly bells the while a-ringing
  'Peace, good-will to men on earth'.

    Gloria in excelsis Deo! . . .

*French, 18th century,
tr. George Ratcliffe
Woodward (1848–1934)*

*A version of 'Angels, from
the realms of glory' (no. 5).*

---

91   *Silent night, holy night!*

1 Silent night, holy night!
  All is calm, all is bright
  Round yon virgin mother and child.
  Holy infant so tender and mild,
  Sleep in heavenly peace,
  Sleep in heavenly peace.

2 Silent night, holy night!
  Shepherds quake at the sight:
  Glories stream from heaven afar,
  Heavenly hosts sing: Alleluia,
  Christ the Saviour is born!
  Christ the Saviour is born!

*Joseph Mohr
(1792–1884), tr. Anon.*

*Franz Gruber composed
this haunting tune for the
newly written German
words (see no. 94) on
Christmas Eve in 1818;
when it was sung that
same night, it was
accompanied only by a
guitar, because by a piece
of poetic synchronization,*

3 Silent night, holy night!
  Son of God, love's pure light,
  Radiance beams from thy holy face
  With the dawn of redeeming grace,
  Jesus, Lord, at thy birth,
  Jesus, Lord, at thy birth.

*the organ had broken
down, making the night
silent indeed.*

---

92   *Sing lullaby!*
 (The Infant King)

1 Sing lullaby!
  Lullaby baby, now reclining,
  Sing lullaby!
  Hush, do not wake the Infant King.
  Angels are watching, stars are shining
  Over the place where he is lying:
  Sing lullaby!

2 Sing lullaby!
  Lullaby baby, now a-sleeping,
  Sing lullaby!
  Hush, do not wake the Infant King.
  Soon will come sorrow with the morning,
  Soon will come bitter grief and weeping:
  Sing lullaby!

3 Sing lullaby!
  Lullaby baby, now a-dozing,
  Sing lullaby!
  Hush, do not wake the Infant King.
  Soon comes the cross, the nails, the piercing,
  Then in the grave at last reposing:
  Sing lullaby!

4 Sing lullaby!
  Lullaby! is the babe a waking?
  Sing lullaby!
  Hush, do not stir the Infant King.
  Dreaming of Easter, gladsome morning,
  Conquering death, its bondage breaking:
  Sing lullaby!

*Sabine Baring-Gould
(1834–1924)*

*Sabine Baring-Gould
wrote most of his best-
known hymns for
children, like 'Onward
Christian soldiers', at
Horbury Bridge, where he
was curate. This lullaby
contrasts the sweetly
sleeping baby with the
sorrow and bitterness that
lie ahead of him, but ends
rejoicing that on Easter
morning he will conquer
death.*

   *The tune is a Basque
noël.*

---

93   *Sing this night, for a boy is born in*
 Bethlehem
 (Star Carol)

1 Sing this night, for a boy is born in Bethlehem,
  Christ our Lord in a lowly manger lies;
  Bring your gifts, come and worship at his cradle,
  Hurry to Bethlehem and see the son of Mary!

John Rutter

*Words and music © John
Rutter. Used by*

See his star shining bright
In the sky this Christmas night!
Follow me joyfully;
Hurry to Bethlehem and see the son of Mary!

2 Angels bright, come from heaven's highest glory,
Bear the news with its message of good cheer:
'Sing, rejoice, for a King is come to save us,
Hurry to Bethlehem and see the son of Mary!'

See his star shining bright . . .

3 See, he lies in his mother's tender keeping;
Jesus Christ in her loving arms asleep.
Shepherds poor, come to worship and adore him,
Offer their humble gifts before the son of Mary.

See his star shining bright . . .

4 Let us all pay our homage at the manger,
Sing his praise on this joyful Christmas night;
Christ is come, bringing promise of salvation;
Hurry to Bethlehem and see the son of Mary!

See his star shining bright . . .

*permission of Oxford
University Press.*

*Although, like 'Deep peace
of the running wave to
you' (no. 20), this would
normally be too difficult
for an untrained
congregation or group of
carol singers to tackle,
John Rutter has made a
simplified arrangement
for this book.*

*This is one of several
works which have broken
through from the
exclusive world of four-
part choirs to that of
congregational hymn-
singing through popular
broadcasting.*

---

94 *Stille Nacht, heilige Nacht!*

1 Stille Nacht, heilige Nacht!
Alles schläft, einsam wacht
Nur das traute, hochheilige Parr.
Holder Knabe im lockigen Harr,
Schlaf' in himmlischer Ruh,
Schlaf' in himmlischer Ruh!

2 Stille Nacht, heilige Nacht!
Hirten erst kundgemacht,
Durch der Engel Halleluja
Tönt es laut von fern und nah:
Christ, der Retter, ist da,
Christ, der Retter, ist da!

3 Stille Nacht, heilige Nacht!
Gottes Sohn, O wie lacht
Lieb' aus deinem göttlichen Mund,
Da uns schlägt die rettende Stund,
Christ, in deiner Geburt,
Christ, in deiner Geburt!

Joseph Mohr (1792–1884)

*The original German
version of 'Silent night,
holy night!' (no. 91).*

---

95 Tell out, my soul, the greatness of the Lord

1 Tell out, my soul, the greatness of the Lord:
Unnumbered blessings, give my spirit voice;
Tender to me the promise of his word;
In God my Saviour shall my heart rejoice.

2 Tell out, my soul, the greatness of his name:
Make known his might, the deeds his arm has done;
His mercy sure, from age to age the same;
His holy name, the Lord, the Mighty One.

3 Tell out, my soul, the greatness of his might:
Powers and dominions lay their glory by;
Proud hearts and stubborn wills are put to flight,
The hungry fed, the humble lifted high.

4 Tell out, my soul, the glories of his word:
Firm is his promise, and his mercy sure.
Tell out, my soul, the greatness of the Lord
To children's children and for evermore.

Timothy Dudley-Smith
(b. 1926)

Words © Timothy Dudley-Smith. Used by permission.

A paraphrase of the New English Bible version of the Magnificat in St Luke's gospel, this hymn has won wide acceptance, and has a good tune, 'Woodlands', written in 1919 by Walter Greatorex (1877– 1949). It should be sung with vigour.

96 The angel Gabriel from heaven came (Gabriel's Message)

1 The angel Gabriel from heaven came,
His wings as drifted snow, his eyes as flame;
'All hail', said he, 'thou lowly maiden Mary,

Most highly favour'd lady,
Gloria!

2 'For known a blessèd Mother thou shalt be,
All generations laud and honour thee,
Thy Son shall be Emmanuel, by seers foretold,

Most highly favour'd lady,
Gloria!'

3 Then gentle Mary meekly bowed her head,
'To me be as it pleaseth God', she said,
'My soul shall laud and magnify his holy name.'

Most highly favour'd lady,
Gloria!

Sabine Baring-Gould
(1834–1924)

Words © in this version Word & Music/Jubilate Hymns.

A carol from the prolific pen of Sabine Baring-Gould (see 'Sing lullaby!', no. 92), who was also a collector of folk-songs.
The tune is an arrangement by C. E. Pettiman (1866–1943) of a Basque noël.

4 Of her Emmanuel, the Christ, was born
In Bethlehem, all on a Christmas morn,
And Christian folk throughout the world will ever
say:

'Most highly favour'd lady,
Gloria!'

---

97 The first good joy that Mary had (The Seven Joys of Mary)

1 The first good joy that Mary had,
It was the joy of one;
To see the blessèd Jesus Christ
When he was first her son.
When he was first her son, Good Lord;

And happy may we be;
Praise Father, Son and Holy Ghost
To all eternity.

2 The next good joy that Mary had,
It was the joy of two;
To see her own son Jesus Christ
Making the lame to go.
Making the lame to go, Good Lord;

And happy may we be; . . .

3 The next good joy that Mary had,
It was the joy of three;
To see her own son Jesus Christ
Making the blind to see.
Making the blind to see, Good Lord;

And happy may we be; . . .

4 The next good joy that Mary had,
It was the joy of four;
To see her own son Jesus Christ
Reading the Bible o'er.
Reading the Bible o'er, Good Lord;

And happy may we be; . . .

5 The next good joy that Mary had,
It was the joy of five;
To see her own son Jesus Christ
Raising the dead to life.
Raising the dead to life, Good Lord;

And happy may we be; . . .

English traditional

*Sometimes called 'Joys
Seven', this is another very
popular folk carol, printed
on broadsheets and sung
all over 18th- and 19th-
century England.*

*W. J. Phillips, in Carols,
wrote that he remembered
in 1850 seeing the
unemployed tramping
through the London snow
with shovels, singing to
this tune 'We've got no
work to do-oo-oo'.*

6 The next good joy that Mary had,
   It was the joy of six;
   To see her own son Jesus Christ
   Upon the crucifix.
   Upon the crucifix, Good Lord;

   And happy may we be; . . .

7 The next good joy that Mary had,
   It was the joy of seven;
   To see her own son Jesus Christ
   Ascending into heaven.
   Ascending into heaven, Good Lord;

   And happy may we be; . . .

---

98 *The first Nowell the angel did say*

1 The first Nowell the angel did say
   Was to certain poor shepherds in fields as they lay;
   In fields where they lay, keeping their sheep,
   On a cold winter's night that was so deep:

   Nowell, Nowell, Nowell, Nowell,
   Born is the King of Israel.

2 They lookèd up and saw a star,
   Shining in the East, beyond them far:
   And to the earth it gave great light,
   And so it continued both day and night:

   Nowell, Nowell, Nowell, Nowell, . . .

3 And by the light of that same star,
   Three wise men came from country far;
   To seek for a king was their intent,
   And to follow the star wheresoever it went:

   Nowell, Nowell, Nowell, Nowell, . . .

4 This star drew nigh to the North-west;
   O'er Bethlehem it took its rest,
   And there it did both stop and stay
   Right over the place where Jesus lay:

   Nowell, Nowell, Nowell, Nowell, . . .

5 Then entered in those wise men three,
   Full reverently upon their knee,
   And offered there in his presence
   Both gold and myrrh and frankincense:

   Nowell, Nowell, Nowell, Nowell, . . .

English traditional

*'Nowell', the old English
form of the French noël, is
a traditional expression of
joy at the birth of Jesus.
The carol tells the whole of
the Christmas story,
combining both Luke and
Matthew.*

*The tune is so familiar
and well-loved, few people
realize how very peculiar
it is. It has been suggested
that it might originally
have been a descant to a
tune that has been lost.*

6 Then let us all with one accord
Sing praises to our heavenly Lord,
That hath made heaven and earth of naught,
And with his blood humankind hath bought:

Nowell, Nowell, Nowell, Nowell, . . .

---

99 *The great God of heaven is come down to earth*

1 The great God of heaven is come down to earth,
His mother a virgin, and sinless his birth;
The Father eternal his Father alone:
He sleeps in the manger; he reigns on the throne:

Then let us adore him, and praise his great love:
To save us poor sinners he came from above.

2 A babe on the breast of a maiden he lies,
Yet sits with the Father on high in the skies;
Before him their faces the seraphim hide,
While Joseph stands waiting, unscared, by his side:

Then let us adore him, and praise his great love; . . .

3 Lo! here is Emmanuel, here is the Child,
The Son that was promised to Mary so mild;
Whose power and dominion shall ever increase,
The Prince that shall rule o'er a kingdom of peace:

Then let us adore him, and praise his great love: . . .

4 The Wonderful Counsellor, boundless in might,
The Father's own image, the beam of his light;
Behold him now wearing the likeness of man,
Weak, helpless, and speechless, in measure a span:

Then let us adore him, and praise his great love: . . .

5 O wonder of wonders, which none can unfold:
The Ancient of days is an hour or two old;
The Maker of all things is made of the earth,
Child is worshipped by angels, and God comes to
birth:

Then let us adore him, and praise his great love: . . .

*Henry Ramsden Bramley
(1833–1917)*

*A carol with magnificent
words, using a series of
striking contrasts to
emphasize the difference
between God's awesome
greatness and the frail
helplessness of the little
human baby that
contains him: 'The
Ancient of days is an
hour or two old'.*

*'A Virgin Unspotted' is a
traditional English folk
carol tune. It can be
effective to sing one or
more verses solo.*

100 *The holly and the ivy*

1 The holly and the ivy,
    When they are both full grown,
    Of all the trees that are in the wood,
    The holly bears the crown:

    O, the rising of the sun
    And the running of the deer,
    The playing of the merry organ,
    Sweet singing in the choir.

2 The holly bears a blossom,
    As white as the lily flower,
    And Mary bore sweet Jesus Christ,
    To be our sweet Saviour:

    O, the rising of the sun . . .

3 The holly bears a berry,
    As red as any blood,
    And Mary bore sweet Jesus Christ,
    To do poor sinners good:

    O, the rising of the sun . . .

4 The holly bears a prickle,
    As sharp as any thorn,
    And Mary bore sweet Jesus Christ
    On Christmas Day in the morn:

    O, the rising of the sun . . .

5 The holly bears a bark,
    As bitter as any gall,
    And Mary bore sweet Jesus Christ
    For to redeem us all:

    O, the rising of the sun . . .

6 The holly and the ivy,
    When they are both full grown,
    Of all the trees that are in the wood,
    The holly bears the crown:

    O, the rising of the sun . . .

*English traditional,
collected by Cecil Sharp
(1859–1924)*

*A very old folk carol,
which Cecil Sharp
collected in Chipping
Campden, and a
reminder that 'carol'
originally meant a dance
accompanied with
singing. It was probably
pagan in origin, the holly
symbolizing the
masculine, and the ivy
the feminine elements,
and the whole being sung
as a dance between the
men and the women.*

101 *The people that in darkness sat*

1 The people that in darkness sat
A glorious light have seen;
The light has shined on them who long
In shades of death have been.

2 To hail thee, Son of Righteousness,
The gathering nations come;
They joy as when the reapers bear
Their harvest treasures home.

3 For thou their burden dost remove,
And break the tyrant's rod,
As in the day when Midian fell
Before the sword of God.

4 For unto us a child is born,
To us a son is given,
And on his shoulder ever rests
All power in earth and heaven.

5 His name shall be the Prince of Peace,
The everlasting Lord,
The Wonderful, the Counsellor,
The God by all adored.

6 His righteous government and power
Shall over all extend;
On judgement and on justice based,
His reign shall have no end.

7 Lord Jesus, reign in us, we pray,
And make us thine alone,
Who with the Father ever art
And Holy Spirit One.

*Scottish Paraphrases
1781, originally J.
Morrison (1750–98),
revised*

*A paraphrase of Isaiah
9.2–7, ending with a
prayer.*

*'Dundee', sometimes
known as 'French', is one
of the most popular and
satisfying of all the
Scottish metrical psalm
tunes, which owe their
effectiveness to their
simplicity.*

---

102 *There'll be a new world beginnin' from tonight (Cowboy Carol)*

There'll be a new world beginnin' from tonight!
There'll be a new world beginnin' from tonight!
When I climb up to my saddle,
Gonna take him to my heart!
There'll be a new world beginnin' from tonight!

1 Right across the prairie,
Clear across the valley,
Straight across every heart and hand,
There'll be a right new brand of livin'
That'll sweep like lightnin' fire
And take away the hate from every land.

Cecil Broadhurst

*Words and music © 1949
The Oxford Group, 12
Palace Street, London
SW1E 5JF.*

*A Moral Rearmament
carol, based on the old
ay-ay-yippee cowboy trail
songs. It has become
popular as one of the high*

There'll be a new world beginnin' from tonight! . . .

2 Yoi, yippee! We're gonna ride the trail!
Yoi, yippee! We're gonna ride today!
When I climb up to my saddle,
Gonna take him to my heart!
There'll be a new world beginnin' from tonight,
From tonight!

points of the famous annual carol concert in the Royal Festival Hall, given by doctors and nurses from London hospitals to raise money for the Malcolm Sargent Cancer Fund for Children.

Coconut shells might provide an appropriate accompaniment!

103 There's a star in the east on Christmas morn (Rise up, Shepherd)

1 There's a star in the east on Christmas morn,
Rise up, shepherd, and follow.
It will lead to the place where the Saviour's born,
Rise up, shepherd, and follow.

Leave your sheep and leave your lambs,
Rise up, shepherd, and follow;
Leave your ewes and leave your rams,
Rise up, shepherd, and follow.
Follow, follow,
Rise up, shepherd, and follow,
Follow the star of Bethlehem,
Rise up, shepherd, and follow.

2 If you take good heed to the angel's words,
Rise up, shepherd, and follow,
You'll forget your flocks, you'll forget your herds;
Rise up, shepherd, and follow.

Leave your sheep and leave your lambs, . . .

American traditional

We might have printed 'foller' instead of 'follow': there is no doubt that the first spelling is closer to the spirit of the piece.

104 The virgin Mary had a baby boy

1 The virgin Mary had a baby boy,
The virgin Mary had a baby boy,
The virgin Mary had a baby boy
And they say that his name was Jesus.

West Indian traditional

Words and music from the Edric Connor

He come from the glory,
He come from the glorious kingdom;
(Yes!) he come from the glory,
He come from the glorious kingdom:
O yes, believer!
O yes, believer!
He come from the glory,
He come from the glorious kingdom.

2 The angels sang when the baby was born,
The angels sang when the baby was born,
The angels sang when the baby was born
And they sang that his name was Jesus.

    He come from the glory, . . .

3 The shepherds came where the baby was born,
The shepherds came where the baby was born,
The shepherds came where the baby was born
And they say that his name was Jesus.

    He come from the glory, . . .

A calypso is a West Indian ballad, sometimes satirical, always topical, usually extemporized to a percussive syncopated accompaniment. In this case it is the story of Jesus' birth that is treated as a piece of topical news.

---

105   *This is the truth sent from above (The Truth from Above)*

1 This is the truth sent from above,
  The truth of God, the God of love,
  Therefore don't turn me from your door,
  But hearken all both rich and poor.

2 The first thing which I do relate
  Is that God did man create;
  The next thing which to you I'll tell
  Woman was made with man to dwell.

3 Thus we were heirs to endless woes,
  Till God the Lord did interpose;
  And so a promise soon did run
  That he would redeem us by his son.

4 And at that season of the year
  Our blest Redeemer did appear;
  He here did live, and here did preach,
  And many thousands he did teach.

5 Thus he in love to us behaved,
  To show us how we must be saved;
  And if you want to know the way,
  Be pleased to hear what he did say.

English traditional, collected by Ralph Vaughan Williams (1872–1958)

A challenging carol musically, this is very haunting and effective in performance, especially as an opening number. Try having a soloist for verse 1, and have your church or hall in complete darkness, gradually increasing the light either by candle power or dimmer switch.

106 'Twas in the moon of wintertime

1 'Twas in the moon of wintertime,
When all the birds had fled,
That God the Lord of all the earth
Sent angel-choirs instead;
Before their light the stars grew dim,
And wondering hunters heard the hymn:

Jesus your king is born,
Jesus is born,
In excelsis gloria.

2 Within a lodge of broken bark
The tender babe was found;
A ragged robe of rabbit skin
Enwrapped his beauty round:
But as the hunter braves drew nigh,
The angel-song rang loud and high:

Jesus your king is born, . . .

3 The earliest moon of wintertime
Is not so round and fair
As was the ring of glory on
The helpless infant there.
The chiefs from far before him knelt
With gifts of fox and beaver-pelt.

Jesus your king is born, . . .

4 O children of the forest free,
The angel song is true;
The holy child of earth and heaven
Is born today for you.
Come kneel before the radiant boy,
Who brings you beauty, peace, and joy.

Jesus your king is born, . . .

*Jesse Edgar Middleton
(1872–1960)*

*A carol in which the
stable is visited by North
American Indian hunters
and braves. Its many
references to the natural
world evoke a strong and
distinctive atmosphere.*

*The traditional French
tune, 'Une Jeune Pucelle',
has been harmonized
here by Frederick Jackisch
(b. 1922). A light
percussion accompani-
ment would work well.*

---

107 Unto us a boy is born!

1 Unto us a boy is born!
King of all creation,
Came he to the world forlorn,
The Lord of every nation, the Lord of every nation.

*Latin, 15th century,
tr. Percy Dearmer
(1867–1936)*

2 Cradled in a stall was he
With sleepy cows and asses;
But the very beasts could see
That he all men surpasses, that he all men surpasses.

3 Herod then with fear was filled:
'A prince', he said, 'in Jewry!'
All the little boys he killed
At Bethlem in his fury, at Bethlem in his fury.

4 Now may Mary's son, who came
So long ago to love us,
Lead us all with hearts aflame
Unto the joys above us, unto the joys above us.

5 Omega and Alpha he!
Let the organ thunder,
While the choir with peals of glee
Doth rend the air asunder, doth rend the air asunder.

You really need some good strong voices to make this one go, to carry the 'Herod then with fear was filled' verse, and an organ that can really 'thunder' also adds to the effect.

The melody, 'Puer Nobis', is in the Piae Cantiones *of 1582, from which so many carol tunes have been taken. The harmony is by G. H. Palmer (1846–1926).*

---

108 Wake! O wake! with tidings thrilling

1 Wake, O wake! with tidings thrilling
The watchmen all the air are filling,
Arise, Jerusalem, arise!
Midnight strikes! no more delaying,
'The hour has come!' we hear them saying.
Where are ye all, ye virgins wise?
The Bridegroom comes in sight,
Raise high your torches bright!
Alleluya!
The wedding song
Swells loud and strong:
Go forth and join the festal throng.

2 Sion hears the watchmen shouting,
Her heart leaps up with joy undoubting,
She stands and waits with eager eyes;
See her Friend from heaven descending,
Adorned with truth and grace unending!
Her light burns clear, her star doth rise.
Now come, thou precious Crown,
Lord Jesu, God's own Son!
Hosanna!
Let us prepare
To follow there,
Where in thy supper we may share.

Philipp Nicolai (1556–1608), tr. F. C. Birkit (1864–1935)

The stirring words, and J. S. Bach's triumphant chorale arrangement 'Sleepers, Wake' of Nicolai's tune 'Wachet Auf', make this one of the grandest carols in any collection. The words and original melody were written at the time of a terrible plague in 1597, and are the fruit of Pastor Philipp Nicolai's profound meditations on the doctrine of eternal life, after 1,300 of his own parishioners had perished. The main biblical references are to Matthew 25, the parable of the wise and foolish virgins.

3 Every soul in thee rejoices;
From earthly and angelic voices
Be glory given to thee alone!
Now the gates of pearl receive us,
Thy presence never more shall leave us,
We stand with angels round thy throne.
Earth cannot give below
The bliss thou dost bestow.
Alleluya!
Grant us to raise,
To length of days,
The triumph-chorus of thy praise.

---

109   *We three kings of Orient are*

(The Kings)

1 We three kings of Orient are;
Bearing gifts we traverse afar
Field and fountain, moor and mountain,
Following yonder star:

    O star of wonder, star of night,
    Star with royal beauty bright,
    Westward leading, still proceeding,
    Guide us to thy perfect light.

(Caspar)

2 Born a king on Bethlehem plain
Gold I bring, to crown him again —
King for ever, ceasing never,
Over us all to reign:

    O star of wonder, star of night, . . .

(Melchior)

3 Frankincense to offer have I;
Incense owns a deity nigh:
Prayer and praising, all are raising,
Worship him, God most high:

    O star of wonder, star of night, . . .

(Balthazar)

4 Myrrh is mine: its bitter perfume
Breathes a life of gathering gloom;
Sorrowing, sighing, bleeding, dying,
Sealed in the stone-cold tomb:

    O star of wonder, star of night, . . .

John Henry Hopkins Jr

*A very successful
Victorian carol — it was
written in 1857 — that
works very well when
staged dramatically: the
three kings, Caspar,
Melchior and Balthazar,
entering in procession
singing the first verse,
then each singing a solo
verse, with the whole
congregation joining in
the choruses.*

(All)

5 Glorious now, behold him arise,
King, and God, and sacrifice!
Heaven sings alleluya,
Alleluya the earth replies:

O star of wonder, star of night, . . .

---

110 *We wish you a merry Christmas (A Merry Christmas)*

1 We wish you a merry Christmas,
We wish you a merry Christmas,
We wish you a merry Christmas
And a happy New Year.

Good tidings we bring
To you and your kin;
We wish you a merry Christmas
And a happy New Year.

2 Now bring us some figgy pudding,
Now bring us some figgy pudding,
Now bring us some figgy pudding
And bring some out here.

Good tidings we bring . . .

3 For we all like figgy pudding,
For we all like figgy pudding,
For we all like figgy pudding,
So bring some out here.

Good tidings we bring . . .

4 And we won't go until we've got some,
And we won't go until we've got some,
And we won't go until we've got some,
So bring some out here.

Good tidings we bring . . .

English West Country traditional

A secular carol, very popular with house-to-house carol singers as a finale — or until the hint is taken. It's worth noting that the chorus begins 'Good tidings we bring to you and your <u>kin</u>', i.e. your family, not your <u>king</u>, which is often sung in error, possibly misread by poor torch light, and because it rhymes with 'bring'.

111 *What child is this, who laid to rest*

1 What child is this, who laid to rest
On Mary's lap is sleeping?
Whom angels greet with anthems sweet,
While shepherds watch are keeping?
This, this is Christ the King,
Whom shepherds worship and angels sing
Haste, haste to bring him praise
The Babe, the son of Mary.

2 Why lies he in such mean estate,
Where ox and ass are feeding?
Come, have no fear, God's son is here,
His love all loves exceeding:
Nails, spear, shall pierce him through,
The cross be borne for me, for you:
Hail, hail, the Saviour comes,
The Babe, the son of Mary.

3 So bring him incense, gold and myrrh,
All tongues and peoples own him,
The King of Kings salvation brings,
Let every heart enthrone him:
Raise, raise your song on high
While Mary sings a lullaby,
Joy, joy, for Christ is born,
The Babe, the son of Mary.

*W. Chatterton Dix
(1837–98) and others*

Words adapted for
English Praise *1975. Used
by permission of Oxford
University Press.*

*The Christmas story told
again, in question and
answer form, this time to
the well-known
traditional English
melody 'Greensleeves',
sometimes attributed to
Henry VIII, and
harmonized here by C. H.
Dearnley.*

112 *While shepherds watched their flocks by night*

1 While shepherds watched their flocks by night,
All seated on the ground,
The angel of the Lord came down,
And glory shone around.

2 'Fear not', said he (for mighty dread
Had seized their troubled mind);
'Glad tidings of great joy I bring
To you and humankind.

3 'To you in David's town this day
Is born of David's line
A Saviour, who is Christ the Lord;
And this shall be the sign:

4 'The heavenly Babe you there shall find
To human view displayed,
All meanly wrapped in swathing bands,
And in a manger laid.'

Nahum Tate (1652–1715)

*Biblical paraphrasing at
its best, by the Poet
Laureate of his day,
Nahum Tate. It is a
paraphrase of the Nativity
story in Luke 2.8–14, and
while respecting the text,
the poet has turned the
story into simple, clear,
singable verse.
    The tune is 'Winchester
Old', first published in
Thomas Este's Psalter
(1592).*

5 Thus spake the seraph; and forthwith
  Appeared a shining throng
  Of angels praising God, who thus
  Addressed their joyful song:

6 'All glory be to God on high,
  And on the earth be peace;
  Good-will henceforth from heaven to earth
  Begin and never cease.'

---

113 *Will you come and see the light?*

1 Will you come and see the light from the stable
    door?
  It is shining newly bright, though it shone before.
  It will be your guiding star, it will show you who
    you are.
  Will you hide, or decide to meet the light?

2 Will you step into the light that can free the slave?
  It will stand for what is right, it will heal and save.
  By the pyramids of greed there's a longing to be
    freed.
  Will you hide, or decide to meet the light?

3 Will you tell about the light in the prison cell?
  Though it's shackled out of sight, it is shining well.
  When the truth is cut and bruised, and the innocent
    abused,
  Will you hide, or decide to meet the light?

4 Will you join the hope alight in a young girl's eyes
  Of the mighty put to flight by a baby's cries?
  When the lowest and the least are the foremost at
    the feast,
  Will you hide, or decide to meet the light?

5 Will you travel by the light of the babe new born?
  In the candle lit at night there's a gleam of dawn,
  And the darkness all about is too dim to put it out:
  Will you hide, or decide to meet the light?

Brian Wren

*Words © Brian Wren
1989. Used by permission
of Oxford University Press.*

*Arrangement © Valerie
Ruddle. Used by
permission.*

*Written for Christian Aid's
'God with Us' booklet, for
the Advent Candle
Ceremony.*

*The Scottish traditional
melody 'Kelvingrove' has
been arranged for this
carol by Valerie Ruddle.*

Index of First Lines and Titles

A child this day is born	1	Il est né le divin enfant	41
A cry in the night	2	I'm standing at windows	42
A great and mighty wonder	3	In a byre near Bethlehem	43
All my heart this night rejoices	4	In dulci jubilo	44
Angels, from the realms of glory	5	Infant holy, infant lowly	45
As Joseph was a-walking	6	*Infant King, The*	92
As with gladness	7	In the bleak midwinter	46
A virgin most pure	8	I saw three ships	47
Away in a manger	9	It came upon the midnight clear	48
Ballad of the Homeless Christ	2	It was on a starry night	49
Bethlehem, of noble cities	10	I warm my son upon my breast	50
Born in the night	11	I wonder as I wander	51
Brightest and best	12	Jesus, good above all other	52
Calypso Carol	89	Jesus, Son of God	53
Cherry Tree Carol	7	Jesus was born in a stable	54
Child in the manger	13	Joseph, dearest Joseph mine	55
Child of Mary, newly born	14	Joy to the world	56
Christians awake!	15	King Jesus hath a garden	57
Come, come, come to the		Les anges dans nos campagnes	58
manger	16	Light, scattering the darkness	59
Come, they told me	17	Little donkey	60
Come, thou long-expected Jesus	18	*Little Drummer, The*	17
Coventry Carol	65	Little Jesus, sweetly sleep	61
Cowboy Carol	102	Lo! he comes with	
Dans cette étable	19	clouds descending	62
Deck the hall	20	Long time ago in Bethlehem	63
Deep peace	21	*Lourdes Hymn*	79
Ding-dong, ding	22	Love came down at Christmas	64
Ding dong merrily on high	23	Lully, lulla, thou little tiny child	65
Every star shall sing a carol	24	Magnificat anima mea dominum	66
Gabriel's Message	96	Make straight in the desert	67
Gaelic Blessing, A	21	Make way, make way	68
Gallery Carol	87	Mary had a baby	69
Georgie	42	*Mary's Boy-Child*	63
Girls and boys, leave your toys	25	Masters in this hall	70
Gloria, gloria in excelsis Deo	26	*Merry Christmas, A*	110
God rest ye merry	27	*Nkosi Jesus*	50
Good Enough for Him	54	No crowded eastern street	71
Good King Wenceslas	28	Now the holly bears a berry	72
Go, tell it on the mountain	29	O come, all ye faithful	73
Hail, Mary, full of grace	30	O come, O come, Emmanuel	74
Hail to the Lord's Anointed!	31	Of the Father's heart begotten	75
Hark! a herald voice	32	O leave your sheep	76
Hark, the glad sound!	33	O little one sweet	77
Hark! the herald angels sing	34	O little town of Bethlehem	78
Here we go up to Bethlehem	35	O Mary most holy	79
He smiles within his cradle	36	Once in royal David's city	80
Hills of the North, rejoice	37	On Christmas night, all	
Holy Child	38	Christians sing	81
How brightly shines the		On Jordan's bank	82
Morning Star	39	O Tannenbaum!	83
How lovely on the mountains	40	*Our God Reigns*	40

O worship the Lord in the beauty of holiness!	84	The first good joy that Mary had	97
Past three a clock	85	The first Nowell	98
People, look East	86	The great God of heaven	99
Rejoice and be merry	87	The holly and the ivy	100
Rise up, Shepherd	103	The people that in darkness sat	101
Rocking	61	There'll be a new world	102
Sans Day Carol	72	There's a star in the east	103
See amid the winter's snow	88	The virgin Mary had a baby boy	104
See him lying on a bed of straw	89	This is the truth sent from above	105
Seven Joys of Mary, The	97	*Truth from Above, The*	105
Shepherds in the field abiding	90	'Twas in the moon of wintertime	106
Silent night	91	Unto us a boy is born!	107
Sing lullaby!	92	*Up! good Christen folk*	22
Sing this night	93	Wake, O wake!	108
Star Carol	93	We three kings	109
Starry Night, A	49	We wish you a merry Christmas	110
Stille Nacht	94	What child is this	111
Sussex Carol	81	While shepherds watched	112
Tell out, my soul	95	Will you come and see the light?	113
The angel Gabriel	96	*Word of Life, The*	43
		Zither Carol	25